H. NORMAN WRIGHT

WHEN THE PAST WON'T LET YOU GO

HARVEST HOUSE PUBLISHERS
EUGENE, OREGON

Unless otherwise indicated, all Scripture quotations are from the Holy Bible, New International Version®, NIV®. Copyright © 1973, 1978, 1984, 2011 by Biblica, Inc.® Used by permission. All rights reserved worldwide.

Verses marked NLT are taken from the *Holy Bible,* New Living Translation, copyright © 1996, 2004, 2007, 2013 by Tyndale House Foundation. Used by permission of Tyndale House Publishers. Inc., Carol Stream, Illinois 60188. All rights reserved.

Verses marked AMP are taken from the Amplified® Bible, copyright © 1954, 1958, 1962, 1964, 1965, 1987 by The Lockman Foundation. All rights reserved. Used by permission. (www.Lockman.org)

Verses marked TLB are taken from The Living Bible copyright © 1971. Used by permission of Tyndale House Publishers, Inc., Carol Stream, Illinois 60188. All rights reserved.

Verses marked NASB are taken from the New American Standard Bible®, © 1960, 1962, 1963, 1968, 1971, 1972, 1973, 1975, 1977, 1995 by The Lockman Foundation. Used by permission. (www.Lock man.org)

Verses marked MSG are taken from THE MESSAGE. © by Eugene H. Peterson 1993, 1994, 1995, 1996, 2000, 2001, 2002. Used by permission of Tyndale House Publishers, Inc.

Verses marked GNT are taken from the Good News Translation in Today's English Version—Second Edition Copyright © 1992 by American Bible Society. Used by permission.

Italics in Scripture quotations indicate author's emphasis.

In the author's examples that draw on interactions with clients, their names and some details have been changed to protect confidentiality.

Cover by Lucas Art and Design, Jenison, Michigan

WHEN THE PAST WON'T LET YOU GO

Copyright © 2016 H. Norman Wright
Published by Harvest House Publishers
Eugene, Oregon 97402
www.harvesthousepublishers.com

ISBN 978-0-7369-6679-5 (pbk.)
ISBN 978-0-7369-6680-1 (eBook)

Library of Congress Cataloging-in-Publication Data

Names: Wright, H. Norman, author.
Title: When the past won't let you go / H. Norman Wright.
Description: Eugene : Harvest House Publishers, 2016.
Identifiers: LCCN 2016006054 | ISBN 9780736966795 (pbk.)
Subjects: LCSH: Loss (Psychology)—Religious aspects—Christianity. | Regret—Religious aspects—Christianity. | Suffering—Religious aspects—Christianity.
Classification: LCC BV4909 .W76 2016 | DDC 248.8/6—dc23 LC record available at https://lccn.loc.gov/2016006054

All rights reserved. No part of this publication may be reproduced, stored in a retrieval system, or transmitted in any form or by any means—electronic, mechanical, digital, photocopy, recording, or any other—except for brief quotations in printed reviews, without the prior permission of the publisher.

Printed in the United States of America

21 22 23 24 / VP-SK / 10 9 8 7 6 5 4 3

Contents

Are We Our Past?

The past—our lives are built on it. Perhaps a better word for it is "foundation." Who we are today is also built on our experiences, as well as conscious and not-so-conscious memories. Some people have used their pasts as launching pads for where they are in present life. They've put their experiences and memories to good use. God's Word says, "When I was a child, I talked like a child, I thought like a child, I reasoned like a child. When I became a man, I put the ways of childhood behind me" (1 Corinthians 13:11).

It isn't necessary to dredge up every experience in our lives to move forward. But it is important to understand the connection between who we are today and the influence of our past because they are intertwined. As a seasoned counselor and crisis responder, I've seen many people who left parts of themselves behind because they'd served their usefulness. At the same time, other portions of their pasts were still influencing, dictating, or controlling their present life—and not always in positive ways. Many of those I see lack the tools to change or aren't aware of how much their pasts are robbing them of a vibrant present and future.

> The past was never designed to limit our present and future.

When we don't move on from the past, our lives might be stunted or stuck, which means we're living as though the past is our present and our future. This is not as it was meant to be emotionally or spiritually. If the past is dictating today or tomorrow, it may be our own doing or we are hanging on to people and significant life experiences. The past was never designed to limit our present and future, yet this is exactly what has happened to many. To cast off negative anchors and sail forward, we need to consider three factors—our past, our present, and our future—and how they interconnect. As believers, we're called to grow in Christ by stepping forward in faith, but sometimes our past acts like a restraining anchor. Anchors have their place and can be useful, but they need to be the right kind of anchor.

One of the small ponds I fish in has massive weed growth as summer approaches. A bell-shaped anchor works well since it doesn't catch the weeds. An anchor shaped like a grappling hook can gather up to twenty pounds of weeds. There have been times when it was almost impossible to lift that anchor. I was stuck.

There are different responses to the past. Some believe it is of little consequence. It has no influence or power in current life. The problems of the past have nothing to do with our choices today. What happened back then has no impact on today or tomorrow. They give it little if any regard in their life. Problems stay in the past and have no influence on today.

Others believe the past is everything, and we should examine every experience under a microscope to get all the nuances. Any failure or problems today can be attributed to the past. Our past wounds haven't totally healed, so they impact our present and our future. We're driven by our past and our need to confront it. Today's poor choices are not our fault. Consider these two possibilities in more detail:

> Some people will never get beyond the pain from their past. It will wreak havoc in their personal and professional lives because they will keep cursing their pain, and it will keep cursing them back. They will choose to believe they are inseparably attached to their past without realizing they are, in fact, making a choice to hold on.
>
> They will hold on to it in one of two ways. Either they will give in to it with a self-loathing that ensures perpetual misery and failure, or they will wage an angry and desperate

war against it in an effort to bury its devastation in self-denial. Either way, they will never surrender the past pain. They will hold on to the idea that they shouldn't have had to go through the pain and that life is not fair. And they will, therefore, miss out on the brand-new ending that could in fact be theirs.

Then there's a group of people who will have taken a different path. They will realize their past isn't really their past. They will come to grips with the fact that their past pain is still impacting them and choose to rise above it... They will surrender their pain. Instead of ignoring or denying it, they will choose to be emptied of it, and in a glorious miracle, God will actually use the pain of their past to help redeem others, in effect, allowing them to find purpose in the pain.

This choice isn't easy. You have to choose to do something you think you can't do. It requires a resolve that can only be found deep within your soul. But this choice does nothing less than determine your destiny.

It's the choice to let go of your desire to have life go the way you planned it. It's the choice to find hope in your hurt. It's the choice called surrender.

There is strength in letting go. There is a radical power in surrender.[1]

I've talked with those who quote Paul's statement in Philippians 3:13-14: "Brothers and sisters, I do not consider myself yet to have taken hold of [righteousness]. But one thing I do: Forgetting what is behind and straining toward what is ahead, I press on toward the goal to win the prize for which God has called me heavenward in Christ Jesus." They focus on the phrase "forgetting what is behind" as meaning we need to do just that. Forget it. Don't waste time on it. Move on. We don't need to give it any attention—except that's not what Paul meant. Paul was simply saying that none of his former righteous deeds could be used as reasons he should be accepted into God's family on his own merit. Salvation is based on God's grace. His former actions were not the basis for his salvation. That's the part of the past he was choosing to forget.

Jimmy Evans describes it this way:

> The Apostle Paul was able to forget the past, not because of his desire to be an emotional martyr or his ability to erase his memory. Rather, he could forget his past because it was reconciled in Christ. The people who had harmed him had been forgiven; the events of his upbringing were dealt with, and every other significant thing in his past had been successfully resolved by the power that only Jesus Christ could give.[2]

The past is not the past until it has been reconciled in Christ. We have to face the past to confront the present. It isn't easy; it can be painful. Many people are reluctant to "face the unacceptable," as Dr. David Hart describes:

> Many people fear that if they face the unacceptable they will become it. The exact reverse is true. If you do not face it, you will become it. It will always be lived out in one way or another. The turning point comes when something in us decides that the unacceptable is really meant for us, and we begin to look for its meaning.
>
> If, on the other hand, we employ our usual means not to face what is meant for us—and each of us has his own particular escapes—the terror of the unacceptable not only remains with us, but is also always being lived out as a real disturbance in our lives. We then need constant reassurance that "it is not really so," a precarious and unreal base on which to live.[3]

You and I are products of the past as is everyone. But many live in the expectation of the future. For many, these two times are permanent. Do you ever wonder why we waste so much time not living in the present? "Many are distracted by the *there and then* rather than the *here and now*."[4]

Consider the thoughts of a man whose past could have destroyed him:

> We bear the imprint of the past as it is, not as it might have been. What actually happened is irreversible, and so are the consequences.
>
> In that sense we are powerless. We can spend the rest of our days reviewing and wishing and imagining and scheming, but we will never be able to alter what has already happened. The past is simply there, influencing everything we do. The best we can do—in fact, the only thing we can do—is remember the past and respond to it.[5]

Jerry Sittser puts it beautifully:

> The past is out of reach; we can neither return to it nor reverse it. It holds power over us because it is unchangeable, rolling over us like waves, one consequence following another. It creates the conditions of the present, whether we like it or not. Still, we have the power to choose how we remember and respond to the past, which enables us to engage the present moment in a redemptive way.[6]

Wouldn't it be wonderful if there was a way to fill the emotional deficits of our pasts and our lives without continuing the risk of experiencing again the disappointment and losses? Well, there is. And it's actually risk free.

I've often heard counselees say they wish they could either erase the past or restore what went wrong. Many wish they could overcome what they consider a wasted past. The past is a part of our life, and it can be used to make the present different.

> It starts with redemptive memory, which enables us to remember the past differently—not as an ideal to which we would like to return or as a regret we would like to reverse, but as one chapter in a larger redemptive story we continue to live out in the present moment. God is in the past,

however ideal or horrible; he rules over the past and promises to use the past, *as it is,* to work redemption. He makes all things serve his plan and fulfill his redemptive purpose.[7]

What it comes down to is that, for many, the baggage of the past can be summed up in one word: hurt. It could have been physical, mental, emotional, or spiritual. I've had a number of counselees say, "Norm, I really don't want to look at all the hurt. What good does it do? I'm past it and ready to move on. I don't want to dredge it up again." But that's why so many people are stuck in their past. Hurt does not stand alone or exit by itself. Hurt is like a cell that mutates and expands. It's like a splinter that constantly festers.

Often it is difficult for us to admit that our hurt occurred. I've heard a number of reasons why some don't want to face their old wounds.

- Some don't want to admit that what happened to them actually happened.

- Some believe if they admit to the hurt and pain of the past, they are in some way different or damaged and not useful to others. They want to see themselves as okay, but they don't. They definitely don't want others to know to avoid being judged or offered unwanted advice.

- Some are afraid to confront the painful past. That's understandable. There is fear that experiencing the pain again might be too much to bear.

- There is also the fear that confronting the past may require change, which opens the door to failure.

The reality is that to move from being a yesterday person to a tomorrow person, we need to admit we were hurt, face it, describe it, and tell our stories. This also means facing what our hurt has turned into—anger.

The word "denial" is overused and probably misused as well. But many of us were taught to deny our feelings. We also deny because, at the time of our trauma or hurt, we needed help to cope. We weren't prepared to experience what was occurring or the feelings that were activated. We pretend what is happening isn't happening and, even if it did, it doesn't matter and won't happen again.

We learn to tune the pain and hurt out like adolescents tune out parental lectures. Think about it. When we experienced our hurt, we were probably too hurt, too shocked, or too young to handle or understand what was occurring. Here's the problem: It's quite easy to turn the pain and hurt on, but it's a lot harder to turn them off. The more we engage denial, the easier it is to resort to it. Denial leads to rationalization and excuses:

> Denial is a general anesthetic. When you numb one emotion, you numb them all. When you flush away your bad feeling, the good ones go down the drain, too. Consequently, it is impossible to *genuinely* feel bliss or any other positive emotion while pushing down pain from the past. Lost joy, excitement, and peace of mind are part of the price you pay for your one-way ticket away from unpleasant realities.
>
> Even though denial is so easily activated and even though you have so many convincing reasons to maintain it, your denial defense system eventually stops working. The feelings you buried periodically rise up from their graves. Memories of old injuries and injustices come back to haunt you, and when they do, your internal defense mechanisms alone can no longer protect you.[8]

Many of us have pasts so wracked with pain that our pattern of life is devoted to playing it safe and, thus, not run the risk of being hurt again. We find ways to create a safe distance and avoid losses, as well as build walls to keep others out. The ways we manifest this vary. We may be aloof, defensive, negative, sarcastic, cynical, or very selective in what we share. We may relate with some people, but we don't make ourselves vulnerable. This brings to mind a phrase in *Why Am I Afraid to Tell You Who I Am?* by Father John Powell: "I'm afraid to tell you who I am because if I tell you who I am you might not like who I am and that's all I've got."

Conversely, our pain may cause us to respond in a totally different way. We may be so desperate for closeness that we go to any extreme to have this false or exaggerated intimacy be a part of our life. We make choices that aren't healthy.

The hurts of the past keep us from the joy of the present and the future.

> Regardless of the approach any of us take or the type of wall we build, the result is the same. We end up feeling lonely, isolated, trapped in a holding cell of our own creation. We wanted to keep people from getting close enough to hurt us. We believed that was what we had to do to survive. But when all is said and done, when all the barriers to closeness have been constructed and cemented into place, we realize we have also kept people from getting close enough to love us, to care about us, comfort us, encourage us, and provide us with the sort of emotional support we need to lead a full and fulfilling life. Once again, we experience pain when pain is precisely what we were hoping to avoid.[9]

I like what Stephen Viars said about four possible ways of looking at our past. We have an *innocent past*. This past is "comprised of the times when you suffered because someone sinned against you or because of trials you faced as a result of living in a sin-cursed world." And this is when we responded *well*.

We also have an *innocent past* when we responded *poorly*. Often we are caught off guard. "We usually aren't prepared for mistreatment, injustice, or abuse. Even when we expect such treatment it hurts. Too frequently, our response to such treatment displeases God" and others. We use sarcasm, revenge, the cold shoulder.

There is also the *guilty past* when we *responded well*. "The guilty past is made up of those occasions initiated by our own wrongdoing. The problem would have never occurred were it not for our sin [not responding properly]."

Finally, we have a *guilty past* when we *responded poorly*. "Sometimes we strike out twice. Not only did our sin initiate the conflict but our next choices made things worse."[10]

Our Past

So, how do we view the past? Do we see it as something more positive in our life or more of a negative? Do we use it as something that has shaped our life for the better or has it been more destructive? Do we see it as a friend or is it one of our worst enemies?

Any hurt we've experienced has to be resolved. When we don't, it festers and stays alive in a detrimental way. Any hurt or trauma that is unaddressed becomes a negative in our life. Viars wrote:

> You probably have distinguishing features—surgical scars, birthmarks, whatever they might be. They are just part of who you are.
>
> Your past is like that. It has marked you, and in some cases, marked you deeply. If you are like most people, you probably don't think about it very much. Your past is a silent companion that accompanies you wherever you go.
>
> What was God thinking? He could have made us without the capacity to remember. Every day would literally be a new day with no memories, no past and no baggage.
>
> Would that make life better? If you could walk through a device similar to a metal detector at an airport but one that would erase your past and its effects on you today, would you do it? And would you be better off?
>
> Some people seem to think so. They describe the past with phrases such as "toxic past," "wounded inner child," or "damaged emotions." In many cases they do so with good reason.
>
> But does it mean that the past, in its entirety, is a bad thing? Would we all be better off if we could completely erase our memories and the impact our past has on our lives today?
>
> Not if we allow God's Word to guide us.
>
> The Bible gives us several ways our pasts can be among our best friends.[11]

James had been coming for counseling for several months. One day during his session, he said, "I've been searching for the right words to describe how I'm feeling and what's going on inside of me. Sometimes I leave here and think I just didn't really describe what's going on inside of me. This week as I was reading Scripture, I found the words. I was reading 1 Samuel 17 about David. In verse 11, I found it: 'On hearing the Philistine's words, Saul and all the Israelites were dismayed and greatly afraid.' That describes me exactly." I've heard many people describe their lives in this way.

I find it interesting that David's response to the challenge drew on what he'd done and learned in his past.

> David said to Saul, "Your servant has been keeping his father's sheep. When a lion or a bear came and carried off a sheep from the flock, I went after it, struck it and rescued the sheep from its mouth. When it turned on me, I seized it by its hair, struck it and killed it. Your servant has killed both the lion and the bear; this uncircumcised Philistine will be like one of them, because he has defied the armies of the living God. The LORD who rescued me from the paw of the lion and the paw of the bear will rescue me from the hand of this Philistine."
>
> Saul said to David, "Go, and the LORD be with you" (1 Samuel 17:34-37).

David used his past experiences in a positive way. He had a choice just like we do as we look at the past: "What have we learned that we can use today in a positive way?" or "What can we take from the past that will hinder us?" David was also a man who experienced multiple traumas, but he drew on what he'd learned to succeed in the present. He benefited from his past.

Do you remember the story of Joseph? (See Genesis 37–50.) Joseph was favored by his father and at odds with his older brothers, who were filled with jealousy. One day they beat him up, threw him into a pit, sold him into slavery, and let their father believe Joseph was dead.

Joseph had quite a past—one filled with hurt, rejection, trauma, and injustice. And it continued. As a slave, he was falsely accused, imprisoned, and forgotten for a long time. When he was finally released, he helped the Pharaoh and was elevated to second in command of the country. When his brothers came to buy food, Joseph revealed who he was. He said, "You intended to harm me, but God intended it for good to accomplish what is now being done, the saving of many lives" (Genesis 50:20).

Joseph didn't try to deny the past. He didn't pretend his brothers had never hurt him deeply. Joseph had grieved the past and worked through it with God's grace so he didn't transfer the pain to his present or future.

I believe two of the most important words in the Bible are "But God." This phrase is used throughout Scripture as a turning point, a line of demarcation between peril and rescue, chaos and control, fall and redemption, hurt and healing.

- The psalmist in Psalm 73:26 NLT: "My health may fail, and my spirit may grow weak, *but God* remains the strength of my heart; he is mine forever."

- Jesus in Matthew 19:26 NLT: "Humanly speaking, it is impossible. *But with God* everything is possible."

- The apostle Paul in Acts 13:29-30 NLT: "When they had done all that the prophecies said about him, they took him down from the cross and placed him in a tomb. *But God* raised him from the dead!"

Once we were dead in sin, *but God* made us alive. Once we were captive to our past, *but God* made us free. Once we were unworthy, *but God* promised to spend eternity unwrapping the riches of His grace in kindness toward us.

A New Way

There's no way around the past. No matter how hard we try, we can't erase it. Our goal is not to become a person who doesn't have a history—that's impossible and useless. The goal is to find a new way of working with the past so it doesn't continue to negatively impact today and our future. The goal is to fight the inner urge we all have to return to the past.[12]

A Helpful Exercise

One tool I've used to help people handle the negatives in their pasts is to help them identify and clarify how their past has controlled them. People sometimes resist some of these statements of admission. Yes, they are quite specific, and sometimes we may need to revisit the statements in order to recall similar situations in our lives.

Take a piece of paper and write down each statement, allowing plenty of room for writing. You may even want to use a separate page for each question. Once you have completed a question, read it out loud as is or put it in the form of a prayer and ask God to continue His healing work in your life.

Statements of the Past

- In the past I was hurt by [name of person] and hurt in this way:
- What he or she did still hurts me in this way:
- What happened was wrong for these reasons:
- The way I've suffered since then is…
- Here is how it continues to impact me:
- Here is what I would like to hear from him or her:

Now, here are some questions to help us move from the past to the present and then to the future. We may find it beneficial to discuss these with our trusted friends.

1. What are some personal habits you would like to modify or eliminate? In what way will this help you become more of a today and tomorrow person?
2. Consider your relationships with friends, relatives, and

coworkers. How would you like these to improve or
develop?

3. What are some changes you would like to make at home,
work, and church, as well as personal, including physical,
mental, and spiritual?

4. What are two problems you would like to resolve in the
next six months?

5. Describe the feelings and emotions you would like to
experience each day.

6. What positive affirmations will you say to yourself just
before you go to sleep and the first thing when you
awaken? Keep paper and pen by your bed to keep track of
how you are feeling and thoughts that come to mind. Ask
yourself about the significance of these responses.[13]

Don't be discouraged if you draw some blanks at first or if your
responses are minimal. If you've been stuck in your past, it will take
some time to shift your thinking.

Some people have found it helpful to write a monthly letter to themselves describing what they did and experienced the previous month.

These snapshots can expose your inner self. You may be required to
face the ugliness, selfishness, and meanness of your own actions. Then
what? In this case, there are no second chances. You are left only with
a bitter memory of failures or the guilt of the good intentions you had
but failed to live up to. Thankfully, God promises to forgive us when
we confess our failures. He will absolve us when we repent, confess our
guilt, ask for forgiveness and, when possible, make right what we have
done or failed to do.

Pat Layton, in her book *Life Unstuck*, suggested six reasons for looking at the past in order to move forward.

1. *God heals what is revealed.* Healing the past begins with
sharing your story with someone you trust…When we
share our past…we begin the healing process to life unstuck.

2. *Covering up versus cleaning up...* When we cover up, we end up stuck.

3. *We pass on what we have not cleaned up.* We must consider the importance of the past and recognize the role it plays in the future and what it may be able to tell you about yourself. In your passage through life, you want to be fully in charge of the route, the events, the destination; in order to do so, you need a clear view of where you have been.[14]

4. *The Holy Spirit gives us the strength to make peace with our past.*

5. *Biblical truth is the key to life unstuck.* The truth contained in the Bible transforms us, but we also need to know there is another *reason* God gave us His Word. "The Bible is not an end in itself, but a means to bring men to an intimate and satisfying knowledge of God."[15]

6. *Freedom comes from surrender.* Allow this journey of looking backward to be the way God begins His amazing healing in your life.[16]

When we give our pain to God, He sets us free.

Remember, there is no perfect solution. We may wish our lives will turn out to match our dreams and that there will be complete healing and positive changes. We can't change others or all the factors existing in our environment. We need to carve out a new normal for us. We need to focus on making internal changes. Look for what is possible and realistic rather than the unobtainable ideal.[17]

Chapter 2

Memories

Years ago, we were entertained by a movie called *Ghostbusters*. Viewers enjoyed the plot and the actors' antics. Some people believe in ghosts and their ability to haunt houses. Some believe they have their own personal ghosts that haunt them. I've heard many say that their memories of the past haunt them. I remember how Tony explained his struggle: "I feel as though I'm haunted—and it's my memories that are haunting me. Some days it feels as though I'm drowning—not in water, but in an ocean filled with flashbacks, intrusive thoughts, and even fears. They vary from fleeting thoughts to 'it just happened.'"

"Haunted" is an interesting word. It can mean "inhibited or frequented by ghosts"; or "preoccupied, as with an emotion, memory, or ideas"; or "disturbed; distressed, or worried." So many people feel their lives are haunted by thoughts and memories over which they have no control. As one woman described them, "What memories I have can best be described as dark. They're destructive. They're bad. They're a source of contamination. They override all that could be good in my life." When I ask counselees what they want, it's often, "I want my bad memories to disappear." It's that simple.

I've been asked, "Can't you do something about these memories to get rid of them?" My clients want me to function like a giant eraser. Short of severe trauma, I don't think there is such a thing as a memory eraser. Memories can be dulled by chemical substance use, but that is temporary and eventually causes more problems. Some individuals vacillate between a "rid the memory" agenda to a "just forget the past"

agenda. Within some Christian circles, a common response to people dominated by the past is Paul's admonition recorded in Philippians 3:13 (NLT): "Forgetting the past and looking forward to what lies
ahead…" I like what Robert D. Jones said about what is possible since
our goal as believers is Christlikeness: "The good news is that if you
belong to Jesus, God does have something better for you. God does not
want to *remove* your memories; he wants to *redeem* them. He wants to
transform them into something good, something that will make you
more like Jesus." Your memories can be opportunities for growth. Jones
said, "You do not need to avoid, run from, cover over, or get rid of your
past. God's goal is neither memory erasure nor memory denial."[1]

Years ago, our country was entertained by a man named Bob Hope.
He was a famous comedian and actor. He entertained United States
military through the USO all over the world. He always concluded his
act by singing a song called "Thanks for the Memories."

Our lives are based on memories. Without them, life is incomplete.
Over time, memories fade or get hazy. They lose their sharpness. We
may need photos or someone's reminder to activate them. Sometimes
sights, sounds, and smells can bring up memories that affect us more
than we want. Anyone who has experienced a trauma, such as an accident, witnessing a violent death, or abuse have memories that when
activated can immobilize, create panic, or bring back all the powerful
feelings from when the event actually occurred.

The terrible reality of severe trauma is that it often eradicates the
existence of positive, healing memories. We're all dependent on positive memories to encourage, inspire, comfort, delight, and heal us.
Memories of having been loved. Memories of having been a success.
Memories of pleasure. Without these and other healing memories, we
remain raw and broken. Very often, a victim's answer to the question
"When were you last happy?" is "Never" or "I don't remember." The
fact that their lives can be different from the brokenness and pain of the
moment isn't remembered or realized; therefore, achieving that pain-
free state isn't considered an option. The task of healing, then, is in part
recovering memories that are healing in nature.[2]

Memories are not just random thoughts. They exist for a reason.

The bottom line is their purpose is to positively influence the present and future based on what we've experienced in the past. How does this occur?

> Your memory creates your future. That's because you imagine the future through the neural networks created by your past. It was true for the Hebrews, and it is true for you today.[3]

Memories can serve at least two purposes. They can be very helpful for our present and future or they can hinder our present and future. When we learn from the past and make positive adjustments, growth occurs. But traumatic and painful memories can bring the past into our present and future in unhelpful ways.

Memories are storage containers. One of the strongest aspects of human memory is the storage of *emotional* experiences. We remember emotions more than accurate facts.[4]

Memories are not literal descriptions of our world. They are really *reconstructions* that are assembled from brain activity. Memories are not facts, although they can be influenced by facts. Our memories can even change without us being aware of it.[5]

There is another aspect to memory that could impact all of us—memory loss. This can occur at any age, although it tends to go hand in hand with aging. Many live with a fear of this occurring from dementia or Alzheimer's, but it's also currently believed to be a natural part of the aging process.

> To move past memory pain, we need to make peace with what happened.

The loss of memory is one of our most important obstacles. Without memory we're limited. When our memory is severely impaired, we are no longer ourselves. Memory is one of our most precious abilities. Without memory, we have no background or way to move forward. Memory is a crucial part of our existence.

There is not just one kind of memory. For example, we have parent memories. These pictures might be a reflection of who we are today.

They contain the emotions we had as a child. This emotion is just as important as the memory itself. When we activate memories, we must be careful not to fall into the trap of using them to blame others for our current emotions. Remember, all of us are flawed. There are neither perfect parents nor perfect children. We all have a condition called "sin." And God loves us despite it. He wants us to grow spiritually, and in doing so we can become emotionally and relationally healthy. If we have set either parent on a pedestal, that needs to change too. Idealizing a parent leads to disillusionment and hurt.

Most of us have voice mail because we want to make sure we don't miss any messages. Some people have call waiting and will interrupt a current conversation to answer so they don't miss the other message.

There are some messages, however, that we wish would disappear. They are in our trauma memories. They float in and out of our minds automatically, and when they invade, they disrupt our lives. The messages are often based on parental interaction since they were the first significant people in our lives. Often the memory is experienced through the inflections of the parent's voice. These memories are often interpreted as truth. Their range is incredible, and may include:

- "You're no good."
- "You're not pretty and never will be."
- "You're a failure."
- "You'll always be fat."
- "You'll never measure up."
- "No one will want you."
- "You can never please anyone."
- "What you feel isn't important."
- "You can't trust your feelings."
- "You can do anything."
- "You are such a special child."
- "I am so proud of you."

Why should we bother dealing with negative memories about

our parents? To move past memory pain, we need to *make peace with what happened.* I've talked with too many people who have denied the impact of their past, which limited their ability to heal and move forward. As our parent memories unfold and are identified, life changes can occur. These memories affect the way we relate to others, how we see ourselves, and how we perceive God.

Memory is made up of bits and pieces of our experiences. They are not just factual events. It's more like a jigsaw puzzle that includes feelings, images, perspectives, and fragments. We spread them on a table and piece them together for our life story. This history can be used to help us make sense of our lives. It doesn't matter who our parents were; it matters who *we remember* they were.

"Time heals all wounds" is not necessarily true. Time by itself isn't a healer. And depending on what we do during that time, our pain could grow if negative thoughts are fed and intensified. But when we put time together with reconciling, distance, and new life experiences, the intensity of some of the feelings and the desire for payment may be blunted.

I remember many childhood memories as pictures. I still see them in my mind. Some I remember as facts having been told them by others. What is the first memory you recall? How we view our past today was shaped by what we collected and stored away as children. A disadvantage is that those experiences were also interpreted by us as children—with a child's way of thinking. Sometimes how we are today is marred by the way we viewed people based on our interpretation of the past. And all of this reinforces your memories.

Dan Allender said, "Memory is to some degree a reconstruction of the past that is highly susceptible to erosion, bias, and error. It is a mistake to consider one's memory completely accurate, no matter the level of emotional intensity or detail associated with the memories. We should maintain a tentative, open, and non-dogmatic view toward all our memories."

Consider this:

> We sometimes think of memory as the mind's safe-deposit

box, a place where we deposit valuables in the form of remembered experiences. Just as we might head to the bank to open the locked metal container where we store our grandfather's solid-gold watch, so we might think that when we want to remember an event, we simply go to our brain's safe-deposit box to retrieve the event we want to examine. When we do, we assume it will be there, unchanged from when we last thought of it.

But memory is in fact *not* like that locked metal box. Every time we remember something, the memory itself changes, for the neural networks that are associated with that mental image are either reinforced to fire in a similar but slightly different fashion or they are shaped and altered to fire differently.[6]

Memories start with an experience, but we often "update" them based on images formed and shaped by the intensity of emotion. Details are altered and some parts are reinforced and intensified while other parts are diminished. All the pieces go together and, for example, form our attitude toward our parents. As an attitude forms, we naturally search for other memories to fit that attitude. Many discount what they thought were facts for a version of what happened or what they experienced based on a memory.

Old hurts, which seemed huge and insurmountable at one time, often recede to the back burner after a number of years as we gather new experiences in life; we frequently view the old ones from a different perspective when we are open to the changing landscape. Our lives can expand in ways that previously seemed impossible.[7]

Memory shapes and controls our lives more than we can grasp. The writers of Scripture knew the value of remembering:

- [God said,] "I will remember my covenant with you and

with all living creatures. Never again will the floodwaters destroy all life" (Genesis 9:15 NLT).

- "Remember that you were slaves in Egypt and the LORD your God redeemed you. That is why I give you this command today" (Deuteronomy 15:15).
- "Remember, LORD, your great mercy and love, for they are from of old" (Psalm 25:6).
- "[Jesus] took bread, gave thanks and broke it, and gave it to them, saying, 'This is my body given for you; do this in remembrance of me'" (Luke 22:19).

Early Recollections

What's your first memory? How old were you? I've heard some amazing stories over the years of memories people have from age four, three, and even two.

Let's begin with your first memories.

My first three memories are:

My age:
Memory:

My age:
Memory:

My age:
Memory:

My first memory of my parents:

My age:

Memory:

As I think about this, I feel…

My best memory I have from my childhood:

My age:

Memory:

As I reflect on this memory, I feel…

My worst memory I have of my childhood:

My age:

Memory:

As I reflect on this memory, I feel…

Often our memories of loved ones are intensified after their death. We're usually encouraged to write what we remember to share with others.

Recollections of our loved one take on greater importance. We preserve their memory. And it is good for us to write down these memories as we recall them, to preserve them for future generations.

But remembrance goes deeper than this. "The biblical notion of remembrance extends far beyond nostalgic recall," scholars tell us. Disciplined remembrance is institutionalized in biblical faith because we are called to interpret our present circumstances in light of God's known faithfulness in the past.[8] Forgetfulness is seen in Scripture as a spiritual malady. If we forget our past, we lose direction for the future because we will forget that we are part of a larger story that God is writing throughout human history.[9]

Why all this emphasis on memory and remembering? Because we're created with the ability to remember. There are good things and experiences we want to hang on to. There are painful things to remember that help us know how to cope or change for the present and future. Remembering has value. How many times a day are we influenced and impacted by our memories? Frederick Buechner is an insightful author who wrote *A Room Called Remember.* He said:

> To remember my life is to remember countless times when I might have given up, gone under, when humanly speaking I might have gotten lost beyond the power of any to find me. But I didn't. I have not given up. And each of you, with all the memories you have and the tales you could tell, you also have not given up. You also are survivors here. And what does that tell us, our surviving? It tells us that weak as we are, a strength beyond our strength has pulled us through at least this far, at least to this day. Foolish as we are, a wisdom beyond our wisdom has flickered up just often enough to light us if not to the right path through the forest, at least to a path that leads forward, that is bearable. Faint of heart as we are, a love beyond our power to love has kept our hearts alive.[10]

In what ways have we survived? What is that strength and what is that wisdom? It is Jesus, the source of everything we need!

> There is no escaping it even if we want to, or at least no escaping it for long, though God knows there are times when we try not to remember. In one sense the past is dead and gone, never to be repeated, over and done with, but in another sense, it is of course not done with at all or at least not done with us. Every person we have ever known, every place we have ever seen, everything that has ever happened to us—it all lives and breathes deep in us somewhere whether we like it or not, and sometimes it doesn't take much to bring it back to the surface in bits and pieces.[11]

We all think and behave in ways we shouldn't. We violate our standards, our societies' laws, and God's laws. Sometimes we beat ourselves up again and again for how we've failed, how we've done, what we know we should have done. God calls it "sin." So do we. Just like trauma, we allow what we've done to dominate our lives. We don't need to do that. It's actually easier and quicker to get rid of the effects of sin than to eliminate the symptoms of trauma. I like the way Max Lucado describes this in *God Came Near:*

> It was when I used the word "remember" that it hit me…
>
> God doesn't just forgive, he forgets. He erases the board. He destroys the evidence. He burns the microfilm. He cleans the computer…
>
> No, he doesn't remember. But I do, you do. You still remember. You're like me. You still remember what you did before you changed. In the cellar of your heart lurk the ghosts of yesterday's sins. Sins you've confessed; errors of which you've repented; damage you've done your best to repair.
>
> And though you're a different person, the ghosts still linger. Though you've locked the basement door, they still haunt you. They float to meet you, spooking your soul and

robbing your joy. With wordless whispers they remind you of moments when you forgot whose child you are…

Poltergeists from yesterday's pitfalls. Spiritual specters that slyly suggest, "Are you really forgiven? Sure God forgets most of our mistakes, but do you think he could actually forget the time you…?"

…Was (God) exaggerating when he said he would cast our sins as far as the east is from the west? Do you actually believe he would make a statement like "I will not hold their iniquities against them" and then rub our noses in them whenever we ask for help?…

You see, God is either the God of our perfect grace…or he is not God. Grace forgets. Period. He who is perfect love cannot hold grudges. If he does, then he isn't perfect love. And if he isn't perfect love, you might as well put this book down.

But I believe in his loving forgetfulness. And I believe he has a graciously terrible memory.[12]

Creating a Memory Room

Some memories are close to the surface. Many memories are deeply buried. Even so, they can still dictate the present and future without our awareness. This is why we need to resurrect memories of the past. I've had numerous individuals say they would like to deal with the trauma and move on, but they're unsure of what to do.

I ask if they have a "memory room," and as yet no one has said, "Yes." Creating one may help. What is it? Actually, anything you want it to be. It will look different to every person, so the initial step is to visualize this in your mind. Imagine a room that contains everything we need to recall to build our histories and identify what is influencing our present and future. To access this room, we don't rely on our own resources. This is a time to ask Jesus to guide and direct us. A simple prayer might be:

Dear Lord,

I have so many memories, some good and some bad. There are some I can retrieve at a moment's notice, but others seem to be locked in a massive vault. I ask You to open the door to help me face the memories so I can rejoice over those that are good and bring the others to You for healing. Show me which ones need to impact my life in a positive way and those that are just there. I ask You to transform my memories and my thoughts so they glorify You and help me.

In Your name, I pray. Amen.

The memory rooms we create are ours alone. It's private and safe. We are in control. Some have said they create a key for this room so they're the only one who can go in and out. Make the room as comfortable as you can.

Another way to access memories is through prayer and writing. Some people sit down and just begin to write. Some write autobiographies starting at preschool age. You may find these phrases helpful starters:

- Memories I am only vaguely aware of are…
- A memory that is hard for me is…
- When I was [age], I…
- Memories I'd rather avoid are…

We all experience memory lapses, and it's not just because we're getting older. We search for what we know, but it can't be found. We can't retrieve what should be retrievable. Sometimes fear wipes out what we know. In 1 Kings 18:19-41 and 1 Kings 19, we read how Elijah, God's prophet, prayed and God answered in a dramatic way. Fire fell from heaven and destroyed the pagan priests. It was an overwhelming display that had never been seen before. *It was unforgettable!* This display by God should have impacted Elijah in such a way that no human threat would bother him.

But one woman made a threat that overrode Elijah's confidence.

Elijah was terrified of the woman's power, so he fled! He had diffi-culty remembering all that God had done to show His power. Instead of remembering the good that had occurred, Elijah focused on what could happen, what might happen. He created a pessimistic future. Basically, he saw himself killed in the future.

God's interaction with Elijah after this failing is interesting. God didn't berate or scold the man or tell him what to do or solve his prob-lem. No, God simply asked in a gentle whisper, "What are you doing here?" In His own way, He was reminding Elijah that he wasn't alone. He was asking Elijah to look at how he was remembering his memo-ries. He was helping him create a new end to his story. He was helping him "remember" his future differently. He asks, "What are you doing here?" And each time there is an opportunity to tell the story differ-ently. The question is repeated because each time we can think differ-ently, change our memories, and remember what the real answers are, as well as the way we remember and live our future.[13]

So, what do we do with memories? In moving beyond the past, it helps to see where we are now and to accept that. The word is "accept," not "resign" ourselves to less than we want. To accept means "to receive with consent." There's nothing about a contract or promise to keep anything forever. You can still reach for anything you want, change anything you like. When you accept this moment, you free yourself to move in any direction you choose. You avoid using energy to fight what has already happened. "What has already happened" doesn't care what we think about it. It just is.

Let's respect our relationship to the past as we experience it now. We carry memories and beliefs with us. Those memories and beliefs can guide us. They can heal us and nurture us, or they can torture and kill us. We often view new events through the same system that took us in that direction in the first place. What occurs then validates our conclu-sions from the past because that's how we see things.[14]

Ultimately, remembrance is not merely backward-looking. Remem-brance as a spiritual discipline gives us strength to live in the pres-ent and direction to move forward. When our future seems uncertain, remembrance of God's past trustworthiness gives us hope to carry on.[15]

Rewriting Our Autobiographies

If asked by God, "What are you doing here?" what would you say?

Memory healing doesn't mean we no longer remember our past. To begin with, this would deny the very aim we've worked so hard to achieve—remembering everything, including the painful experiences we've previously tried to forget. Also, it would be unscriptural. The Bible doesn't tell us to forget our past in that sense. "Memory healing" means being delivered from the prison of past hurts. We remember but in a different way. *We can't change the facts we remember, but we can change their meanings and the power they have over our present way of living.* Too often, Christians have taken Romans 8:28 out of context. We need to remember just where that great verse appears—it follows two verses about inner healing we quote so often:

> The Spirit helps us in our weakness. We do not know what we ought to pray for, but the Spirit himself intercedes for us through wordless groans. And he who searches our hearts knows the mind of the Spirit, because the Spirit intercedes for God's people in accordance with the will of God.
>
> And we know that in all things God works for the good of those who love him, who have been called according to his purpose (Romans 8:26-28).

A major part of the healing process is the discovery that God can take even the most painful of our experiences and work them out for our good and His glory. As noted before, this does not mean God is the Author of everything that has happened to us. But it does mean He is the Master of it all.

This is where follow-up counseling can be most valuable—to help you discover meaning and purpose in your life. During the follow-up sessions, rewrite your autobiography by seeing and assigning new meanings to even the most painful incidents—the meanings God is going to work through them.[16]

> Remembering, therefore, is not simply a function of the mind. It is an embedded expression of our lives as we recall

the concrete, earthbound actions of God and people. It is
an invitation to grace and adventure that involves all God's
people. It is not just the past in our heads. It is the present
in our doing.

That is why I believe that faithfully telling and listening to
our stories is one of the single most important things we
can do as followers of Jesus. Storytelling inevitably engages
our memories—both the speakers' and the hearers'—and
so opens the door to a different future. The Bible is so powerful in part because it contains the *story* of creation, rebel-
lion, redemption, and recreation, all of which are told in
the rich, messy, beautiful, tragic, hopeful tapestry of the
lives of God's ancient people.[17]

We all have a unique life story. It may be helpful, no matter what
our ages, to write an unofficial autobiography. Writing it in longhand,
although extra work, makes us be more deliberate and requires our
utmost attention. This helps us think and process more slowly. In
doing this, we access both sides of our brain; they will connect and
blend better. We'll be helping our brains integrate our two sides and
function as God intended.

Finding Your Memories

You are looking for memories. Search for the earliest one you can
find. Once you find it, stay in that decade. Write as much as you can
about that time. If a later event arises, write it down and return to it
later. Don't be concerned about proper sequences, writing style, spelling, grammar, and punctuation. You're after memories. Write about
factual events, but don't leave out feelings, images, colors, smells, and
so forth. If something comes to mind and you think, *That's not important*, it probably is so write it down. Do this for each decade of your life.

As you write, your brain and memory will be activated, and you will
most likely remember what you thought was forgotten. This may occur
especially after the next important step. Select someone you trust and
read your story to them. Encourage them to ask you questions. You'll
find your brain coming alive as you engage your memories in this way.[18]

What does memory and remembering have to do with our Christian life and work?

> The past and the future, memory and expectation. Remember and hope, remember and wait. Wait for him whose face we all of us know because somewhere in the past we have faintly seen it, whose life we all of us thirst for because somewhere in the past we have seen it lived, have maybe even had moments of living it ourselves. Remember him who himself remembers us as he promised to remember the thief who died beside him. To have faith is to remember and wait, and to wait in hope is to have what we hope for already begin to come true in us through our hoping. Praise him.[19]

Setting Memory Work Boundaries

I think it's safe to say that at one time or another we've all struggled with sleep. And there's a multitude of reasons. Sometimes it's our memories. On other occasions, it's what we remember or are trying to remember. Yes, there is sleep medication, but this may not be the solution if the sleeplessness cause is residue from the past, an overload of stress and pressure, family issues, worry—and the list goes on. What you watch, listen to, discuss, or think about prior to sleep makes a difference. There is a solution—your thoughts and God's Word. What is suggested here has been the solution for many. And it's simple. Prior to turning out the light, read the following Scriptures aloud. Take your time in doing this. Then read the prayer by Ron Mehl out loud. Now turn out the light.

- "When you lie down, you will not be afraid; when you lie down, your sleep will be sweet. Do not be afraid of sudden fear nor of the storm of the wicked when it comes [since you will be blameless]; for the LORD will be your confidence, firm and strong, and will keep your foot from being caught [in a trap]" (Proverbs 3:24-26 AMP, brackets in original).

- "When you lie down, you will not be afraid; when you lie down, your sleep will be sweet" (Proverbs 3:24).

- "If I'm sleepless at midnight, I spend the hours in grateful reflection" (Psalm 63:6 MSG).

- "When my anxious thoughts multiply within me, Your consolations delight my soul" (Psalm 94:19 NASB).

- "In peace I will lie down and sleep, for you alone, LORD, make me dwell in safety" (Psalm 4:8).

- "In a dream, a vision of the night, when sound sleep falls on men, while they slumber in their beds, then He opens the ears of men, and seals their instruction" (Job 33:15-16 NASB).

Dear God,

We give thanks for the darkness of the night where lies the world of dreams. Guide us closer to our dreams so that we may be nourished by them. Give us good dreams and memory of them so that we may carry their poetry and mystery into our daily lives.

Grant us deep and restful sleep that we may wake refreshed with strength enough to renew a world grown tired.

We give thanks for the inspiration of stars, the dignity of the moon and the lullabies of crickets and frogs.

Let us restore the night and reclaim it as a sanctuary of peace, where silence shall be music to our hearts and darkness shall throw light upon our souls. Good night. Sweet dreams. Amen.[20]

Do the same the next night, but this time pray "God Works the Night Shift" by Ron Mehl after you've read the Scriptures aloud. Alternate these prayers for a month and allow God's Word and these thoughts to impact your brain and thought life.

God Works the Night Shift

He's busy while you slumber. He's into the job while you're into your dreams. He's fully engaged when you've pulled the plug. The psalmist put it like this: "He who watches over you will not slumber; indeed, he who watches over Israel will neither slumber nor sleep" (Psalm 121:3-4).

This is the God who moves outside our vision and occupies himself with tasks beyond our comprehension. His eyes peer into what we can't see; his hands work skillfully where we can only grope. This is the God who reaches and thinks and plans and shapes and watches and controls and feels and acts while we're unconscious under sheet and a comforter.

But don't get the idea that he's off attending to black holes and quasars or fussing with hydrogen molecules in a time-distant galaxy. God works the night shift *for you.*

He's occupied all night long thinking about you. His interest in you never flags or diminishes—not even for a heartbeat. He is busy on your behalf even when you are not aware of it, even when you are doing absolutely nothing. When it comes to your life, he never stops observing, giving, directing and planning. "'For I know the plans I have for you,' declares the LORD, 'plans to prosper you and not to harm you, plans to give you hope and a future'" (Jeremiah 29:11).

And me? Well, I know he's working. I know he's on the job. But lots of times I have no idea what he's doing. To be honest, there are seasons in life when he doesn't seem to be doing much of anything. I stare into the murky darkness of my frustration or grief or confusion, but I can't see a blessed thing.

Sometimes I want to say, "If God is at work in my life, I sure can't see it." But deep down, in my heart of hearts, I know this: Even if there are no Under Construction signs, no tracks from heavy machinery, no sounds of heavenly jackhammers in the background, the Master Architect and Builder is always hard at work in the lives of his children.

God is aware of your circumstances and moves among them.

God is aware of all your pain and monitors every second of it.

God is aware of your emptiness and seeks to fill it in a manner beyond your dreams.

God is aware of your wounds and scars and knows how to draw forth a healing deeper than you can imagine.

Even when your situation seems out of control.

Even when you feel alone and afraid.

God works the night shift.

Dear Lord,

What comfort it gives us to know that you are mindful of everything—everything—that concerns us. You are intimately involved with even the smallest details that affect our souls. May we trust in the Lord, even when our world seems to crumble around us. Let us not forget that you still hold us in the palm of your hand. Amen.[21]

Chapter 3

We Are Our Thoughts

What were you *thinking*!" Remember those words? Perhaps they had this emphasis: "What were *you* thinking?" or even "What *were* you thinking?" Growing up, I heard these words with the various inflections and soon knew what the tone of voice meant. Usually it meant I was in trouble. I had many responses to this statement: "Um...I didn't know," or "Thinking? Who was thinking?" or just silence. That question could have come from our parents or teacher or another adult. Someone was appalled at something we said or did and immediately "thought" something was wrong with us—particularly our thoughts. Perhaps they believed that if we corrected what we were thinking, we would be better people.

Perhaps that's a fair question that you and I ought to ask ourselves from time to time. "What *was* I thinking?" Perhaps it was the culprit for my negative response, so maybe I should have been thinking something different. Our minds are filled with thoughts all day long. Thousands of them. They influence every part of our lives. It's like a massive airport in our brain with thoughts landing, taking off, and taxiing on the runway. Sometimes one gets in the way of another. You're probably (hopefully) having thoughts as you read this.

So what is a thought? Thoughts are made up of memories, perceptions, and beliefs. They're glimpses of ideas. Whether you choose something to think about or you don't, your brain is always on. If you don't choose your thoughts and direct them somewhere, your thoughts will wander. Thoughts are simple. They're basic, but it's hard to measure them.

They direct our lives. They impact our mind, our body, and our emotions. Long and involved or short and direct, they influence our lives.

What we think affects our bodies. In fact, in the next minute what I'm asking you to think about will create a response in your body. Take a couple of breaths and relax. Now, think of a lemon. Imagine cutting the lemon in two. Scrape out a couple of the seeds. Hold the lemon up to your nose and smell it. Squeeze it in your hand, and let some of the juice drip into your mouth. Now bite into it and chew the juicy pulp.

Now, all you did was think about doing this. You didn't really bite into this juicy lemon. But most of us who followed those instructions responded physically. Our mouth may have puckered, our nose may have twitched. The chewing wasn't real, but the thought of doing this revved up our senses.

Our thoughts have tremendous power and influence. They're a mixture of the functioning of our brains and the influence of our pasts. Let me tell you about an experience I had in a counseling session. It began with a question. "So, Norm, where do *you* live?" I looked at Frank for a minute before I responded. This was the first time I'd met him. He'd called for a counseling appointment, and I remembered the conversation well. It was more of a monologue than a dialogue. Frank rambled and seemed to jump from subject to subject rather than getting to the point. I try not to start counseling sessions over the phone, especially when it's to set up an appointment, but I had my hands full this time. When Frank arrived, he looked around my office at some pictures, paintings, and mounted fish. Then he asked where I lived.

I repeated his question and said, "As you probably surmised since you're in my office in my home, I live here in this house, at least most of the time. What part of town do you live in, Frank?"

His answer was not what I expected. "Norm, I live in my head. Yeah, I have a house like you do, but the truth is I live in my head. I live in my thought life. I've been to enough counseling to know that my reality is in my head. I carry on full-blown conversations with others in my head. Probably most of what I do and what I say and how I live my life (good and bad) come from all those thoughts floating around. And I don't think I'm that different from others—even you.

So, if you're going to help me, you need to get into my thought life and do your work there."

Was Frank right or not? Is what he said your experience? Is it mine? Is it universal? For some of us, our minds or thought lives are in constant motion. I heard someone say, "I am my thoughts." Are we? What do we really know about our thoughts?

Thoughts and Emotions

Let's talk about thoughts and emotions. Sometimes we may wonder where they came from. One emotion out of ten is the source of what we were thinking about. If our thoughts were negative, we give our emotions control as well as set up chemical reactions within ourselves that aren't always reliable.

Are you aware that we walk around with a network of electrical chemical switches constantly turning on and off? These electrical impulses are our thoughts. Every thought we have is translated into electrical impulses that direct the control center in our brain. It's taking place right now as we think about what we're reading. We have more power than we realize to control our thoughts. The more we think a thought, the more it becomes entrenched. For example, I can plant roses in my yard. If I feed and water them, I'll have a garden worth looking at. But if I fail to feed them or give them wrong ingredients, my yard won't be worth looking at. It's the same way with thoughts. Our minds are like a bank—a memory bank. We go there constantly to make deposits. When the time comes to make a withdrawal, what will we take out? It's going to be what we deposited. What we plant or file away will come back to either enhance our life or damage it. You and I can limit ourselves just based on our thoughts alone.

When we were passing through childhood and adolescence, what did we often hear from parents and significant adults? Mostly positive statements or mostly negative ones? We've all been influenced in one way or another. How many times did we hear the word "no"? Most of us heard it between 100,000 to 140,000 times and with a multitude of inflections.

Were we usually told what we could do or more what we couldn't do? What impact does that have on our thoughts? For most of us, our thoughts had to contend with the negative, which may have hindered our ability to move forward in some way. The mind is a storehouse of experiences and thoughts that create our foundational beliefs and attitudes. What we tuck away is basically what we're going to use to interpret our world. And for most of us, these beliefs and habits are deeply entrenched. Jesus described this: "What comes out of a person is what defiles them. For it is from within, out of a person's heart, that evil thoughts come—sexual immorality, theft, murder, adultery, greed, malice, deceit, lewdness, envy, slander, arrogance and folly. All these evils come from inside and defile a person" (Mark 7:20-23).

Once unwelcome thoughts pop in, we have the choice to allow them to stay or to evict them. Colossians 3:1-2 NASB helps us: "Therefore if you have been raised up with Christ, keep seeking the things above, where Christ is, seated at the right hand of God. Set your mind on the things above, not on the things that are on earth."[1] "Set your mind" can be translated to "think." There it is. A simple word. "Think." Think can also mean "have this inner disposition."

All of us attempt to change our thoughts. We've tried different approaches or programs, prayed about it, been prayed over, and so forth. But we still struggle. It's not that easy.

If a new thought coincides with what we already believe about ourselves, it will be accepted by us with open arms. If it doesn't, it will have a difficult time finding a place to fit in and be accepted. Isn't it interesting how we even resist thoughts that are new, positive, and in line with biblical thinking? We resist giving up old mental messages because we're comfortable with them, even if they're not the best, not true, not helpful, or keep us stuck in the past. Sound familiar? I'm guilty of doing that. In my office I have filing cabinets filled with files. In my mind, I probably have hundreds of files, and just like the ones in my office, I need to go through them from time to time to clean house. I need to get rid of those I don't use, don't need, and that are detrimental to healthy growth. I have stuff in my office files that reinforces what I think is good, is right, and is truth. Some of it doesn't. It's outdated and inaccurate. It's the same way with the storage of my thoughts. I may think what I have stored in the receptacle of my mind is good, is best for me, is truth—but not all of it is.

Some new information or biblical truth is better, but the longer I've had the other thoughts and beliefs stored away and I've added to them, the more difficult it is to change the old beliefs and let the new thoughts become active in my life. Sound familiar? I'm going to admit something to you. I carry on conversations every day. Yes, I do. I talk to people on the phone. I talk to others face-to-face. I also carry on conversations with myself within the confines of my mind. And this is completely normal.

Our unspoken thoughts can involve words or sensations. I heard one person say, "I'm a thinking machine, and my 'on' button never shuts off." Are you aware of all your inner conversations? Probably not. Sometimes our thoughts and conversations are feelings, which can be difficult to put into words. Some are only partially formed while others are fully thought out.

Our thoughts and pictures in our minds are usually connected to something else we already know. Let's say you have a thought you've never had before. When I'm writing a book such as this one, I will have ideas or thoughts that I've never had before (or at least I don't remember having). When this happens, my brain jumps in and tries to connect the new thought with something already in my brain to help the thought fit. Whatever you think has to fit in somewhere in your mind's storage system.

Making Changes

Sometimes our thoughts interfere with how we function in everyday life. To change thought patterns is not a simple step-by-step process or an overnight event. Our brains weren't designed to make sudden, permanent changes.

The brain follows patterns of established neural connections (habits) built over the years. This unique organ of the body—with its billions of neurons and millions of pathways, circuits, and memory cells—doesn't erase or "write over" what it's stored. So when we begin changing patterns, we should expect the old ways of thinking and talking to challenge the new ways. Change is possible; it just takes time and effort.

Our thoughts influence our character, shape our attitudes, determine our behavior, affect us spiritually, and even influence our immune systems. Our thoughts create emotions that can have lasting physical effects on our bodies. If we dwell on old hurts and wounds, we build a mental habit. That's how the past can dominate the present. Every time we think about that pain from the past, stress—and its toxic effects—surfaces with increasing speed. Each time we think that negative thought, we build a stronger pathway to that negative emotion, and we're more likely to express ourselves in a negative way. Just think of that thought as a cutting tool creating a groove in the brain. Each stroke makes the groove a little deeper, a little more permanent.

The big question is, "Where do our thoughts come from?" Let me share what I call the "Thinking Triad." In this triad, you and I have the following: our memories of the past, our judgments of the present, and our imaginations of the future. All of these create emotional responses. Sometimes we're not even aware of what is taking place inside of us.

Perhaps the big question is, *Where do we spend most of our time?* Some live in their memories of the past—and these could be wonderful, fulfilling memories or they could be laden with pain. They could be sharp and clear or vague and fleeting. If this is where we live, how does that impact our daily life? Does it help us move forward or remain stuck? Think about this. If we had to determine how much of our thought life resides in our memories, what would we say? Yes, it's a strange question and perhaps difficult, but think (there's that word again) about it.

Identify the percentage on the chart that reflects the memories portion of your thought life.

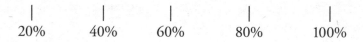

Keep this chart handy and reflect on this throughout the day. Some have been quite surprised.

Now consider your judgments of the present. This is where you're thinking of the here and now. Evaluate this on the same chart:

What about the imaginings of your future? Thoughts in this dimension can draw us forward or keep us immobilized. Often the content reflects the passage in Genesis 6:5: "The LORD saw how great the wickedness of the human race had become on the earth, and that every inclination of the thoughts of the human heart was only evil all the time."

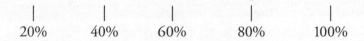

In the past 45 years of counseling, I've seen so many whose thought lives were stuck in the past or their future imaginings were so negative and worrisome they couldn't move forward. I've asked many to keep track of how much of each day is negative, how much is positive, and what thoughts are creating the problem. I remember asking a mother to do this, and I was a bit shocked the next time she came in for an appointment. As she walked into the office, she threw several sheets of paper at me and said, "Here are your stupid papers." After sitting down she sighed and said, "Now I know what's wrong with my life."

For the majority of us, the negative is not what is occurring in the here and now, but it's reaching either into the past for the painful experiences or imagining the worst in the future that might happen. So which of these voices is strongest in your life? Is this voice helping you move forward or stay where you are? There are times when our mind (thought life) is in balance and productive and other times it seems like our worst enemy. Perhaps a good question is, "Where is most of the chatter in our minds coming from?" We all have these voices within us. Some are talkative and seem to shout and control our lives. Others whisper and have little influence. We also have an "interior commentator." What does our commentator say most of the time? Are the thoughts positive and creative and in line with what Scripture says about life and reality? Are they fearful and worrisome?

The Truth About Worry

Worry is a powerful magnet. We get caught up in the "what ifs." Perhaps we're interested in what can go wrong in life. We're fascinated by the possibilities. And when a possibility is discovered, we latch on with all of the "what ifs" our minds can create.

Worry is a special kind of fear. To create it, we elongate fear with two things—anticipation and memory. We then infuse it with our imagination and feed it with emotion. Then we become "our own creation." In its positive sense, anxiety is a God-given instinct that alerts us to fearful situations and prepares us to respond appropriately. But worry can also be like a car alarm system that won't turn off.

Pastor Earl Lee illustrates the difference:

> Worry is like racing an automobile engine while it is in neutral. The gas and noise and smog do not get us anywhere. But legitimate concern…is putting the car into low gear on your way to moving ahead. You tell yourself you are going to use the power God has given you to do something about the situation which could cause you to fret.[2]

Worry immobilizes and doesn't lead to action, while legitimate concern activates us to engage our thoughts to overcome the problem.

There are many diseases in our world today, but worry is an old one—a disease of the imagination. A Swedish proverb says, "Worry gives a small thing a big shadow." Scripture speaks to this problem also: "All the days of the afflicted are bad, but a glad heart has a continual feast [regardless of the circumstances]" (Proverbs 15:15 AMP, brackets in original).

Does our *interior communicator* reflect the positive or negative?

When a negative thought develops, it activates a section of our brain that we're probably not aware of at that moment, and it releases emotions related to the thought. If it's a negative thought, one of those insidious "downer" chemicals is released. But it doesn't stop there. It also stimulates the release of another, which stimulates the release of yet another and so on. We wonder, "What's going on with me?"

Chemicals released by negative emotions affect our brain's nerve cells and cause difficulty in retrieving memories. That, in turn, suppresses the ability to remember and to think in constructive ways. Those who experience a major loss and are in grief or those who have experienced a trauma have even less ability to remember.

Research shows that chemicals released in the brain as a result of positive thoughts don't cause this kind of damage. Test yourself for a half an hour. Write out as many positive thoughts or blessings as you can and then read them out loud. How do you think you'll feel at the end of the half hour?

There is more good news. Our thoughts can also create a calmness that helps control our emotions and rein them in before they spin out of control. Every positive or happy thought spurs our brains to action, releasing chemicals that make us feel good. These help us become a today and tomorrow person and break loose from the past. Take this statement: "I am a today and tomorrow person," and repeat it out loud ten times every day. We'll experience a difference in mood and attitude.

Remember, thoughts follow specific pathways in the brain. They don't bounce around randomly landing somewhere. Each pathway was created for a specific purpose. God created our brains to function this way. This memory stage is similar to a library. It's responsible for the first emotional response to any thought. It activates and arouses us to do something. If our "library" is filled with "books" that tell a story about not being able to cope with the incoming information, the first response will be to rate this information based purely on emotion by activating old memories from the past. That's why it is best not to react to the first emotion you feel.[3] I'm sure people have told you to "check out" and evaluate your first impulse. You've probably told people that too. The past does not have to be your present reaction.

When our thoughts are negative, we risk giving our emotions control. Unless the situation activates balanced thoughts, the emotion it generates can dominate.[4] And the result is not usually the best response. Remember this: The more emotional damage in our past, the more potential damage in our present and future.

This is why our memories, even those we don't consciously recall, have such powerful effects. Like all humans, we carry with us hidden memories. They're stored in our minds, burned into the hard drive. When the "right" key combinations are hit, they're triggered and reappear.

We all have memories hidden beyond our conscious memories,

blocked because the events were extremely painful or traumatic. It's as though we put a lid on something we didn't want to face. The ability to repress emotionally painful material can serve an immediate, positive purpose, but eventually not identifying, recognizing, and dealing with it keeps us stuck being yesterday people.

Let's take this a bit further. Science confirms what Scripture has been saying all along. You and I are shaped, in large part, by our thoughts. The apostle Paul wrote, "Fix your thoughts on what is true, and honorable, and right, and pure, and lovely, and admirable" (Philippians 4:8 NLT). This helps break the chains of the past. After dealing with the trauma, we focus our thoughts on God and His blessings. Our outlook will be changed when we apply Scripture.

The Scriptures have much more to say about the act of thinking and our thoughts. The words "think," "thought," and "mind" are used hundreds of times. "All a person's ways seem pure to them, but motives are weighed by the LORD" (Proverbs 16:2).

God designed us so that our thoughts have an impact on every aspect of life. Positive, healthy thoughts bring about positive effects. Negative thoughts take everything—from attitude to health—in the opposite direction. The author of Proverbs wrote: "A cheerful heart is good medicine, but a crushed spirit dries up the bones" (Proverbs 17:22).

Our thoughts—good and bad—*affect* what we say and do. Jesus said, "A good man brings good things out of the good stored up in his heart, and an evil man brings evil things out of the evil stored up in his heart. For the mouth speaks what the heart is full of" (Luke 6:45).

No one has to be a helpless victim of their thoughts—even if they were stamped on their minds thirty years ago. Again, look at the promises in Scripture. Paul wrote, "God did not give us a spirit of timidity or cowardice or fear, but [He has given us a spirit] of power and of love and of sound judgment and personal discipline [abilities that result in a calm, *well-balanced mind* and self-control]" (2 Timothy 1:7 AMP, brackets in original). Scriptural teachings about our thoughts aren't just informative, they also encourage us. Making Scripture the basis for our lives will help bring us out of the past to experience the joys of the present and the hope for our future.

The first step is repeating the encouraging verse 2 Timothy 1:7 aloud. But we need to go further. How do we see ourselves living this Scripture? What would this mean? Complete this statement: "If I were reflecting a calm and well-balanced mind, I would…"

Remember, though, our brain is used to our old thoughts. What it needs is constant reinforcement from us. Specific directions, words, results, and directives are what we need to help our minds learn a new way of thinking.[5] Our goal is to learn to regard our thoughts as we might watch clouds floating by. Mental events float past, and we see them for what they are—thoughts that aren't necessarily reality. We're to live now and not in the past.

Have you heard the expression "zoned out"? It's quite common. I'm sure you've heard the expression, "She's lost in thought." Often our facial expressions give us away when we've tuned out. "The porch light is on, but no one is home." When we're lost in thought, we're not present. Have you ever been there? I have. Often I can tell which of my students are present during a lecture by observing the expressions on their faces. When we're lost in thought, our minds have taken us out of the present. We're away from our physical presence. We're cut off from connecting with the people around us. We're not in the "here and now."[6] When this happens and we come back to reality, it's like life went on around us but we missed out. I've even had people respond, "Where was I? I sure don't know."

I remember the first time I was consciously aware of this happening to me. It was my first year of college, and I was driving to USC in Los Angeles from Hollywood. I turned onto La Brea Avenue and drove until I had to turn onto another main street. I was thinking or daydreaming because it dawned on me, "I have no recollection of driving the past few miles!" I missed out on a lot, and it was a bit scary. This experience prompted quite a bit of thinking.

Some people feel as if they've been overwhelmed by a flood when emotions from the past hit. It's as though they went to a football game and got so involved they were drawn into the action as participants rather than observers. This can also happen when reading a good novel or watching a movie.

When our thoughts feel like reality, we tend to believe them. It's like traveling with friends. We fall asleep and eventually we wake up and realize we have no idea where we are.

Over the years, I've listened to the efforts of many who struggled to control their thoughts. I've read numerous books on this subject, but I've learned more from counselees. Some try to change their thinking by going elsewhere in their minds. If I suggested you *not* think of the color red, what would happen? That's all you'd think about! One of my counselees, Alice, came up with a practical idea:

> I've been trying to control my thoughts for ten years, and nothing seemed to work. One day I wrote down the thoughts. My sister asked, "If you could summarize your thoughts with one or two words, what would you say?"
>
> So I tried to put a label on my thoughts. This helped. Then, since they came and went like an intrusion, I labeled them as a visit. My sister called them an uninvited, unwelcome, unnecessary visitor. I learned I couldn't keep them from occurring, so I went with them. I put out the welcome mat for them. I learned to say, "Oh, it's you again. Oh well, you've pretty well worn out your welcome and any useful-ness you may have had. You're actually a pain in the neck. But if you want to come in for a while, that's okay. But realize there's no real use for you to stick around anymore. I've got better thoughts now." I know it sounds crazy to carry on this kind of conversation with my thoughts, but it works.

I've found it works for others as well.

Whenever we have negative thoughts or messages from the past, we need to do a little digging. We need to investigate and acknowledge the presence of our intrusive visitors by name or label.

I usually ask counselees, "When unwanted thoughts come, can you stop them?"

"No."

"Can you keep them from occurring?"

"No."

"But you try?"

"Yes."

"Even though it doesn't work, you keep trying?"

"Yes."

"So, if this doesn't work, there's got to be a better way. Let's find it."

"But how?"

There are several steps involved.

First, identify the thought or message. Did this come from our minds or from someone else? Who originated the thought? Is it true? Write down our responses.

Identify whether the thought is based on the past or the present.

Thinking of the relationship between thoughts and emotions, we'll discover that negative thoughts and depression are closely connected. In *Moving Beyond Your Depression*, Dr. Gregory Lantz wrote:

> It is part of the human condition that negative thoughts seem to flow easier than logical and more positive ones. An overactive brain can take a small incident and quickly inflate it into a major crisis. If this pattern is repeated often enough, the person becomes swept away in the mental torrent, unable to find the footholds they used to return to the solid ground of common sense and reality. When the flow of thoughts slows down, the person is able to better realize the truth and maintain a grip on their probabilities.

> If a person is naturally pessimistic, inclined toward runaway thoughts, expression is often the result. The person who feels powerless to control his or her thoughts assumes that the worst that can happen soon will. This focus on disaster does not allow the person to keep optimism, hope or joy, in his or her sights for very long, if at all. Negative self-talk and the grim atmosphere of a foul mood fuel this fatalistic mental spiral.[7]

Does what Dr. Lantz said apply to your life?

Third, welcome the thought. I know this seems odd, but old

messages or intrusive thoughts don't stop when we tell them to. Saying, "Don't come in!" or "Go away!" or "I won't think about you!" doesn't work for most individuals. Instead welcome them. That's right, welcome their presence by saying:

> Well, here you are again. You're a real pain in the neck. I don't like you or want you, but I've handled you before and I'll do it again. You don't have the power or impact you once did. If you're a thought, you're not the truth. You never were. If you're an experience, it's over. I'm moving on. I will acknowledge you, but this time I'm giving you to my Lord Jesus Christ. He is the source of all truth, strength, and wisdom. I will rely on Him to counter whatever you attempt to do to control or influence me.

Whenever a thought, memory, or physiological response from the past occurs, invite it in and then challenge it. Don't accept it as the truth or the end of the journey.

Why does this work? It's simple. It impacts our brains.

It's possible that you and I have more than one mind inside our head. I'm not talking about multiple personalities here. Just that we are capable of having different, even opposing thoughts. Sometimes one of our "minds" is dominated by the other. It could be that our minds carry on warfare between each other. Paul wrote, "The weapons we fight with are not the weapons of the world" (2 Corinthians 10:4). These weapons have divine power to demolish strongholds.

Our different minds have various characteristics reflected in our thoughts. One may be a self-affirming mind. It's kind to us, builds us up, gives us the benefit of the doubt, sees the potential in our lives. But many have a critical mind, which drags them back into past pain. Unfortunately, this mind can contaminate and influence our present as well as our future. I've seen people who let this critical mind have control. They end up believing and reinforcing the old, negative messages.

There's a better way! Replace the old thoughts with truth. Look at the old messages in the light of Scripture. Do these messages, no matter who they are from or when they came, reflect what God's Word says about us? God's is a much better voice to hear. Consider this: When we invited Jesus into our lives something happened. The initial act of saving faith led to a life of faith. The transforming of the mind at salvation started a lifelong process of renewing the mind, and this continues as long as we are breathing. Paul wrote, "Do not conform to the pattern of this world, but be *transformed* by the *renewing* of your *mind*" (Romans 12:2). To the Ephesians, Paul wrote, "Let the Spirit renew your thoughts and attitudes" (Ephesians 4:23 NLT). Jesus, answering the question as to which was the greatest commandment of the law said, "Love the Lord your God with all your heart and with all your soul and with all your *mind*" (Matthew 22:37). Peter also spoke of renewing the mind when he commanded, "Prepare your *minds* for action" (1 Peter 1:13 NLT). Paul called for believers to "set your mind on things above, not on earthly things" (Colossians 3:2).[8] Our minds are "transformed" and "renewed." We need to remind ourselves of this several times a day.

When engaged with our thoughts (including feelings, images, bodily experiences, memories, smells, and brilliant new revelations), let's be sure to return to the Word of God for wisdom. If negative thoughts arise, we need to gently bring our attention back to the truths in the Bible. Again, picture thoughts as if they are on clouds that are floating away or on lily pads floating downstream. We might get lost in negative thought a dozen times, but we can gently bring ourselves back to the Word.[9] We need to keep feeding our minds with Scripture: "I have hidden your word in my heart that I might not sin against you" (Psalm 119:11).

Our Mind Is to Be Alive

God has a plan for our thought life. He has an ideal for us. The New Testament describes or implies what a Christian's mind is to be like: "For the mind set on the flesh is death, but the mind set on the Spirit is life and peace" (Romans 8:6 NASB). When we invite Jesus Christ into our lives, we are made new. We come alive. We show this new life by the choices we make. This change is usually a major adjustment. We're now faced with choices regarding what we think about, what we dwell on, what we put into our minds, what we say, and so forth. I've heard people say, "After I invited Jesus into my life, I felt alive for the first time in my life." But there is also struggle because the new life is such a contrast to the previous life.

Take time to sit and reflect. Are you still struggling with the old thinking pattern, with clutter in your mind? Or is there a sense of being alive in your mind?

Our Mind Is to Be Peaceful

You and I have choices regarding what we focus on in our thoughts. The apostle Paul said:

> For those who are *living* according to the flesh set their minds on the things of the flesh [which gratify the body], but those who are *living* according to the Spirit, [set their minds on] the things of the Spirit [His will and purpose] (Romans 8:5 AMP, brackets in original).

The very next verse tells us, "The mind of the Spirit is life and peace." You and I set our minds. That's our work. The result of doing this is peace, which is God's work. Yes, it may take time, but it's a step in breaking from the past.

There is tremendous power in our thoughts. Our minds are powerful, but whatever thoughts pop up, we can refuse to let them reside in and dominate our lives. Sometimes when we're lost in thought, it's because we're lost in passive thinking. Our thoughts are rambling along with no direction. They go all over the place and are often anything but productive. If our thoughts are negative, they might link up with other negative thoughts that are flitting around and in our memories. We need to watch out. We have a choice between passive thinking or directed thinking. Passive is automatic; directed is on purpose.[10]

In passive thinking we tend to be the passengers of our minds rather than the drivers. Passive tends to look for the negative or the worst in a person or situation. Directed thinking is more in line with biblical teaching and can be a positive in your relationships.

Years ago I read a book entitled *Depression Is a Choice*. There was truth in what the author said, but people were bothered because the book revealed that people do have a choice when it comes to emotions. We don't have to be victims. "Think of depression as a panic room of the mind. It is a chemical state of alarm that we have, somehow, built into a holding room."[11] Many of our emotions are determined by our thoughts. If our thinking becomes anxious, so do our emotions. Reasoning can override emotion. Our mind follows our instructions and will do the kind of thinking we tell it to do.

Certain kinds of thinking can contribute to depression and might even lead to chemical imbalance. Of course, not all chemical imbalances are the result of unhealthy thought patterns but these can be a factor. Ultimately, every thought creates a chemical response.[12]

Depression caused by our thoughts is generated in the emotional part of our brains. The process described here as *brain switching* takes us to the thinking part of our brain that doesn't contain depression. Brain switching creates new neural patterns. This process teaches us to be responsible for our thoughts and actions.

Brain switching is simply changing our thoughts from those that create depression to those that don't. The new thoughts can be anything. It's a matter of selecting thoughts in advance and saying them repetitiously out loud to impact depression. It could be a song, a prayer, a statement, or even a phrase that has meaning only for us. These phrases block what is creating and continuing the depression. For instance, we could repeat, "Yes, I am a child of the King," or "I am learning to overcome worry," or my favorite, "Blue frog." I know this sounds simplistic, but try it. When you're feeling down, select a new phrase and say it out loud fifteen to twenty times. This crowds out the passive and negative thoughts we let flow around in our minds.

How we feel is a choice. What does Scripture say? "Think about all you can praise God for and be glad about. Keep putting into practice all you learned from me and saw me doing, and the God of peace will be with you" (Philippians 4:8-9 TLB). Knowing the steps to change only helps if we practice them. I took piano lessons for ten years and

> We have the ability to change our thoughts.

practiced an hour a day, again and again and again. That's why I can play whenever I sit down at a piano. Some of the practicing was boring and redundant. I wasn't always happy to practice. But now I feel it was worth every moment of training and changing. And changing thoughts is changing the pattern in my brain.

We have the ability to change our thoughts. They are not in charge of our minds or our lives. When we challenge our thoughts—questioning their source and whether they're true—we allow our brains to create new responses and sift through the old information. For this to be really effective, there is a great way to do it: *Speak the words out loud.* Why? Hearing it enhances our ability to think on a higher, more rational level. Hearing our own voices aloud has greater impact on our brains than just thinking the words. We become more aware of the abundance of thoughts we have about people and our relationships. We become more aware of the content of our minds. We're more likely to evaluate our thoughts more thoroughly when we hear them. We may respond, "That really is true!" or we may object, "That's so far from the truth it's ridiculous."

Daily Affirmations

I encourage you to take one month out of your life and spend five to ten minutes a day building a new foundation for your life. Take three times a day to rebuild and counter the negatives you say about yourself. It's only three to four hours over a 30-day period. That's all.

The following thoughts are true and based on Scripture. You can use them as affirmations. Begin by asking God to take these and make them the basis for who you are and how you live. *Read them aloud.* Many of these have been personalized and put in first person so they can come from your heart.

- God said, "You are my creation, my handiwork, my masterpiece. I'm proud of you and what I've done in you."
- "[God] chose us in him before the creation of the world to be holy and blameless in his sight" (Ephesians 1:4).

- I am God's handiwork (Ephesians 2:10).
- "I have engraved you on the palms of my hands" (Isaiah 49:16).
- God, thank You for naming me. I know my name is safe in Your mouth. You know my name! You know me and love me.
- God will never leave or forsake me (Hebrews 13:5).
- God knows and makes plans for me. They are plans to prosper me and not to harm me, plans to give me a hope and a future (Jeremiah 29:11).[13]

God made me to reflect Him just as a mirror reflects an image.
Because of Christ's redemption,
I am a new creation of infinite worth.
I am deeply loved,
I am completely forgiven,
I am totally pleasing,
I am totally accepted by God,
I am absolutely complete in Christ.
When my performance
Reflects my new identity in Christ,
That reflection is dynamically unique.
There has never been another person like me
In the history of mankind,
Nor will there ever be.
God has made me an original,
One of a kind,
A special person.[14]

God takes great pleasure in us. He wants us to live in the present and look forward to a positive future.

Chapter 4

Emotions and Life— Especially Anger

Years ago, I had the privilege of counseling a delightful elderly woman. She came to see me about her struggle with anger. It was soon clear that in Sarah's life, the "secondary" emotion of anger was usually in response to the "primary" emotion of hurt.

As we discussed her story, I asked her about her earliest memory of hurt. She responded immediately. "Well, I was raised on a farm, and our family was quite poor. When I started first grade at the local country school, my parents couldn't afford to buy me dresses so my mother worked hard to make some dresses out of flour sacks. They looked nice, but all the other children knew where the material had come from. They made fun of me." As she told the story of what had happened to her, tears came into her eyes. Sixty-five years later, the pain of that humiliation was still there as vivid as if it had happened yesterday.

Hurt and pain are part of life. Thankfully, they seldom reach out from the past to limit us today. As one author said, "If every name you were called, every test you failed, or every disappointment you experienced still affected you, you would be too paralyzed by pain to get out of bed in the morning."[1]

Significant hurts don't disappear on their own. Hurts and wounds do matter, especially when they interfere with the quality of our present life. It does matter that we were hurt. If it happened, the best step is to face it. Denying it won't work; running from it won't work; burying it with work, food, sex, or substance abuse won't work. Hurt comes in many packages. It could have been rejection, or abandonment, or ridicule, or betrayal, or abuse.

Hurt, like fear, is a very uncomfortable emotion. When we're hurt, we're vulnerable, we're weak and drained, we feel hopeless and helpless. When the pain of hurt is denied and stuffed into the subconscious, we may not think about it but that doesn't mean it has disappeared. "Out of mind" does not mean "out of memory." Eventually the layers of hurt, confusion, and misunderstanding make it more difficult to access the facts and interpretations that caused the hurt. Hurt can remain repressed for years. The pain simmering inside us, if not dealt with, will suddenly boil to the surface, moving past the potentially positive emotion of anger to the damaging emotion of rage.

Hurt is emotionally draining, so we often turn to anger to find the energy to throw up walls to protect ourselves. At first, the walls keep people out and, thus, keep the hurt out. Anger can veil the hurt, fear, pain, and sense of loss from real or perceived rejection. We think, *If no one gets close to me, then no one can hurt me.*

Many people are surprised to learn that hurt and anger go together. People often assume that angry people are so insensitive they must be incapable of being hurt. In truth, the obnoxious person often has experienced deep hurt, typically in childhood. Because we are more likely to be hurt by people who are important to us, we are more likely to feel anger toward those closest to us, especially our family members.

When our hurt comes from another person, we often end up holding something—a grudge. And this drains us because it's fueled by emotional energy. It's an emotional wound we go back to again and again, not letting it heal.

> Indeed, many of us wake up each morning and fill an enormous suitcase with pain from our pasts. We stuff it with grudge, bitterness, resentment, and self-righteous anger. We toss in some self-pity, envy, jealousy, and regret. We load that suitcase with every injury and injustice that was ever done to us, with every memory of how others failed us and how we ourselves have failed, and with all the

reminders of what we have missed out on and what we can never hope to have. Then we shut that suitcase and drag it with us wherever we go.

With so much of our time and emotional energy going into this seemingly endless cycle of pain, smoldering rage, and subtle or not-so-subtle paybacks, we have little left for the good things in life and none at all to make ourselves and our circumstances any better than they are.[2]

Like the tired, irritable, downtrodden traveler, our excess emotional baggage weighs us down, saps our energy, slows our progress, and sometimes even convinces us to cancel the trip—giving up on our goals and aspirations or settling for far less than we planned originally. Up until now, you simply did not know there was any other way to travel.[3]

It's important to learn how to distinguish between hurt and anger. Paul Welter suggests that, for the most part, hurt is the *first* emotion to be felt but the one that is least accessible to memory. Anger is the *second* emotion we experience, and the one we are most aware of.[4] If we ignore the warning sign of anger, it can easily turn into resentment and a desire for revenge.

Anger puts up a wall to protect us from hurt. The short-term effect is that we don't hurt or the pain is dulled. The long-term effect is that the problem we avoided and ran from gets worse. Hurt revisited is always greater than it would have been if we'd used our anger energy to address the problem the first time around. If we allow resentment to have its way, we will remain imprisoned in our past. Resentment will poison our present and ravage our future.

In my counseling work with someone who has a problem with anger, one of the first questions I ask is, "Can you tell me the last time you experienced deep hurt?" Usually they expect me to ask about anger, not hurt. Frequently, people will pause and then tell a story. In many cases, tears will come to their eyes. They may share situations from childhood when their brother or sister was favored. I find it amazing that things that happened twenty or thirty years ago caused a wound that won't heal until we deal with it or until the day we die.

The Value of Feelings

Over the past forty years of counseling, I've learned an abundance of helpful information and insight, but not enough. There is so much more to learn. How did I learn?

I was raised like most men—emotionally handicapped. I wasn't taught much about emotions or how to express them. I never cried. But when I entered into an arena of deep hurt and pain, I learned to free my emotions as well as cry. Matthew helped me become fully human. We all learn through different experiences. My son was born with severe developmental issues. My wife and I experienced loss every day with him, but through this our lives were changed for the better. Matthew was one of the greatest blessings we ever experienced.

I learned the role of feelings, of emotions.

I learned the value of crying, of tears expressed.

I learned the value of sharing words.

Too many individuals stop listening to their feelings. They ignore them, try to make them disappear, or decide they aren't important and can't be trusted. But that's not the way God views emotions. Dr. Gary Oliver describes our emotions in this way:

> When we ask Christ into our hearts, a radical transfor-
> mation takes place. However, the consequences that sin
> has had on our mind, will and emotions do not immedi-
> ately disappear. I believe that an important part of the pro-
> cess of sanctification involves the healing of our damaged
> emotions.
>
> One of the most significant aspects of being a person is that
> we were created in God's image. We bear the image of and
> in specific ways resemble our Creator. Even though the
> image of God in men and women was damaged and dis-
> torted by sin, we are still image-bearers.
>
> When God created us in His image, [He] gave us mind,

will, and emotions. As image-bearers we have the capacity to feel, to think, and to make choices. Francis Schaeffer said that "as God is a person, He feels, thinks, and acts: so I am a person, who feels, thinks and acts."

It is unfortunate that over the years many Christians have emphasized the mind and the will to the exclusion of the emotions. Some are more comfortable with facts than feelings, others with ideas than with people. Many of us have been led to believe that spiritual maturity consists primarily of acquiring facts or head knowledge. The more propositional truth we can cram in our craniums, the more spiritual we will become. Some have taught that if we fill our mind with the "right" information and make the "right" choices, our emotions will take care of themselves and automatically follow right behind.

The obvious implication is that emotions aren't important. Certainly they are not worth paying much attention to. Yet maturity is more than the acquisition of facts and head knowledge.

Head knowledge is important, yet true spirituality is much more than what I know or don't know. True spiritual maturity includes growth and development in the understanding and expressing of emotions.

Emotions are important. Emotions enhance our ability to be in relationship with God and with one another. But due to the Fall and the effect of sin in our lives, our emotions, like our mind and our will, have become damaged and distorted. For many people, the emotions that God gave many people to make life more meaningful, instead make life more miserable.

Our emotions influence almost every aspect of our lives. God speaks to us through our emotions. They are like a sixth sense. Emotions help us to monitor our needs, make us aware of good and evil, provide motivation and energy for growth and change. Emotions give us the vigor, power and impetus for living.

Sin has led to our responding to emotions in one of two unhealthy ways. First, we can deny or ignore our emotions. From this perspective, the intellectual is more important than the emotional. In its extreme form, head knowledge is deified and emotions are suspect.

Second, we can allow ourselves to be controlled by our emotions. This is an equally dangerous position. From this perspective, the intellect is suspect. "If I don't feel it then I can't trust it," say those who embrace emotions exclusively.

By God's grace there is a third option. The healthy response is to view your emotions from God's perspective and to bring them into harmony with your mind.

An important part of the process of sanctification is the healing of our damaged emotions. God wants to help us recover from the effects of sin on this key dimension of our personality, to restore healthy God-designed balance among our ability to think, choose and feel.

When we understand our anger and choose to express it in healthy kinds of ways, it has enormous potential for good.

What a person feels is one thing. What he chooses to do in response to that feeling is another. The very same emotion can be constructive or destructive. The degree to which our emotions help us or hinder us depends on the degree to which we acknowledge them, understand them, choose to channel them through our thought life, and view them from a balanced, healthy perspective.

Many grew up in homes where emotional expression was punished and emotional repression was reinforced. This could have been your experience. If you were raised in this environment, you either consciously or unconsciously told yourself that it wasn't safe to feel. For the sake of survival, your mind was trained to ignore emotions, filter them out, or, when one accidentally crept up to the surface, stuff it back down.

In this kind of environment you weren't free to learn how to experience or express your God-given emotions. The only thing that felt safe was not to feel. And you became emotionally numb.

Our emotions are like tools. It takes time and effort to learn about our emotions. Through trial and error we learn when we can trust our emotions and when we can't.[5]

There is so much in what Gary had to say. Read this again and indicate which statements pertain to you.

If we run away from our feelings, moving on and forward means facing and allowing our feelings to exist and making peace with them. Most of us, at one time or another, tend to squelch them to hold them down, to get away from them. We do this to gain relief from their presence, from the hurt they bring. We try to divert them.

How do you seek relief from strong emotions? Some block them, or eat, or drink, or grab a novel. Instead, think about this: What would it feel like *not* to avoid feelings? What would it feel like not to block them but to encourage them, to feel them? Can we stay put and face our feelings? The more we do this, the more we can move forward. Becoming aware of our "went elsewhere" when we became uncomfortable or afraid of our feelings will help us discover what it's like not to retreat or deny or hide.[6]

We can learn to face and sit with our feelings. Yes, it may be new and feel strange, but we can be safe with them, which will allow us to move from the past to the present, and then on to the future. We can do this!

One of the ways of managing emotions is by labeling them or giving them names. That helps us recognize what we're feeling. Those who write about their intensely emotional or traumatic experiences show improvement in health areas, including healthy brain function. When we label feelings or an emotion, we regulate the emotion in the brain. This can have a calming effect. The more we label and write, the greater control we have to regulate emotions.[7]

Many have found using this *Ball of Grief* helpful in identifying the emotions or feelings they're experiencing. Whenever you experience an emotion, try identifying it with one of these words:

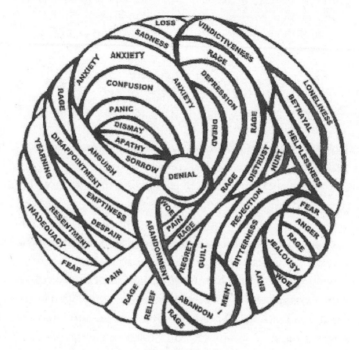

The Ball of Grief

Remember that you have more control over emotions than you realize, whether it be fear, anger, sadness, anxiety, guilt, or depression.

If we welcome emotions, talk with them, and learn from them, we may lower their intensity. Using one of God's gifts—our imagination— picture a volume dial like on an old radio. This is like a "feelings" dial. It has numbers on it from one to ten, from low to the most intense. Look carefully at this dial in your mind. See what it's made of. Imagine how it feels in your hand. Now, select the unpleasant feeling and determine what number reflects how weak or strong it is.

Write down that number. Describe what it is like to be tuning in on that number. What would it be like if the number was on two? Eight?

Somewhere in the middle? If you would like to turn it down, what number would you turn it to?

Now, turn the dial lower until it goes down one number from where you started. Keep turning it down lower and lower and lower. Do it slowly until you find the intensity you want. Go slow and breathe deeply at each number. What is the intensity like when you reach the desired number?

When your feeling intensity is too high, go through this process. When it's lower, you can handle the feelings better and take appropriate action.[8]

Consider the benefits of anger. There is much said in Scripture about anger, both positive and negative. Anger is part of the healing process in grief because it gives voice to our complaints, especially when we've been hurt or impaired. It's a way of saying, "This isn't right. This is wrong!"

If we were fortunate to come from healthy families, we probably experienced accurate information about feeling angry and what to do with it. But many people haven't had that privilege. Of all the unhealthy displays of anger in a home, anger purposely avoided and not expressed can be devastating. Many homes give the appearance of stability and healthy interaction. From all outward appearances, the parents appear calm, consistent, and balanced. But anger exists. You find it in tight lips, piercing looks, punishing silence, and incivility. The children don't express their anger. They don't dare. It's forbidden. They are taught, "Not only do you not show anger, you don't feel it either."

I've had numerous counselors tell me about "the look." Jim told me, "All I had to do was walk into the room and Mom or Dad would give me *the look*. They didn't have to say a word. I got the message, and it tore me apart. I felt their disgust, their contempt. It was a feeling of distaste. I felt like a piece of garbage when I saw their expressions, their scowls. When I was younger I knew what was coming next—*the punishment*." Nonverbal responses can be just as devastating as words that wound.

These children are being taught a life-debilitating pattern of denial. Not just of anger, but of hurt as well. We may have learned this pattern as children. As adults, we may be teaching our children this behavior.

The denial of any emotion leads to an accumulation of it. Soon there is an overabundance with no proper avenue of drainage. Denying an emotion means we have turned its energy back into ourselves. We are slowly destroying ourselves and our potential.

David Viscott, a psychologist and author, describes the consequences of pent-up anger:

> When we hold in feelings, we distort the world around us. We really do not believe what we profess to be true, and so we doubt our judgment. We make villains out of the people we love and begin to lose belief in ourselves as well. We become more interested in being right than in making peace. Although we hold feelings back to stay in control, doing so makes us feel fragile and at risk of going out of control. Our anger builds. We struggle to keep from exploding. We take it out on innocent people. We are easily triggered by minor frustrations.[9]

How can people know about our hurts when all we show them is anger? If I were counseling you, I would say, "Tell me about your anger. Tell me who you are most angry at and why."

You might say, "But I'm not angry."

I will continue my gentle approach until you realize it's safe to admit the anger that has probably built up over the years. Discovering what your anger is about and who it is directed toward keeps you from continuing to direct the emotion against yourself. It allows you to learn tools for handling your emotions and defending yourself. It helps you take the blame that others may have directed toward you and keep it from turning into shame. It also lessens the fear you may have of others and what they've said and done. Anger can be toward others or toward the circumstances you're in.

> People overreacting are usually reacting to a past event.

Often anger builds up over a period of days, weeks, and even months, and then something minor happens at home or at work and there's an emotional explosion. People overreacting are usually reacting to a past event rather than what's going on in the present.

Cindy expressed yet another common difficulty with anger. "You know, there are times when I wonder if I'm angry and don't even know it. Sometimes I get angry, but it seems to take so long to arrive. Rarely does it come when the problem occurs. It's like I have a delayed fuse, and sometimes I don't even know that it's lit until I explode. It's hard for me to experience anger. And I wish it would happen at the time I need it the most."

Many people are like Cindy. They regret lost opportunities to legitimately express their anger. Later on they imagine what they would have liked to have said. They feel it might have been beneficial to have expressed their emotions at the time.

Anger and Guilt

Janice presented a unique conflict over her anger. "It isn't just when I express anger that I feel anger. It's when I feel anger that the guilt starts. I end up feeling miserable over the fact that I get angry. But sometimes I need to be angry, and yet my guilt cripples my anger and keeps it from being productive. Perhaps I'm expecting that I should be more in control of my feelings. I wish I could control my guilt rather than have it control my anger."

There are two kinds of guilt. Some people label them good guilt and bad guilt; others call them legitimate guilt and illegitimate guilt. Guilt that is often out of proportion to an event is the bad or illegitimate type. Feeling this kind of guilt can be normal in a crisis that involves the loss of a significant person and usually it comes from unrealistic beliefs—the "I should haves" that no one can attain.

The person who moves on in life from a trauma talks over his or her feelings with a person holding an objective outlook on the situation. If the only one we're talking to about our guilt is ourselves, we need to remember that we're biased. A nonjudgmental person can help us look at whatever is creating our guilt feelings, whether they be acts, thoughts, or perceived omissions. Another person's rationality can help us evaluate our guilt and keep us from overemphasizing the negative.[10]

As soon as we work through what's going on, we will find our guilt gradually diminishing. And when the guilt tries to creep in, we'll be able to evict it more quickly. When guilt becomes a part of our lives, these questions may help us evaluate it. (I recommend discussing these questions and your answers with a trusted friend.)

- What is the reason for the guilt I feel? Is there something I did or didn't do? If so, what was it? Would anyone else agree that I was truly responsible?

- Is what I did wrong or contrary to God's Word and teaching in any way?

- Is this something I need to make restitution for or confess to anyone besides God?

There may be legitimate or good guilt in your life. Good guilt has a purpose. It shows us where we've gone wrong and what we need to change. It can motivate us to grow. This legitimate guilt (which we might experience in a trauma) happens when there is a direct cause-and-effect relationship. When this kind of guilt happens, we can do something about it. We can admit what we've done, make restitution if possible, and, above all else, confess it and receive God's forgiveness.

God's forgiveness is always available. It can't be bought; we can't work for it. It's a gift from God.

- "I acknowledged my sin to You [LORD], and my iniquity I did not hide; I said, 'I will confess my transgressions to the LORD'; and You forgave the guilt of my sin" (Psalm 32:5 NASB).

- "If we confess our sins, He is faithful and righteous to forgive us our sins and to cleanse us from all unrighteousness" (1 John 1:9 NASB).

- "There was a time when I wouldn't admit what a sinner I was. But my dishonesty made me miserable and filled my days with frustration. All day and all night your hand was heavy on me. My strength evaporated like water on a sunny day until I finally admitted all my sins to you and stopped trying to hide them. I said to myself, 'I will confess them to the Lord.' And you forgave me! All my guilt is gone" (Psalm 32:3-5 TLB).

In its simplest definition, shame is the deep sense that you are unacceptable because of something you did or something that was done to you.

Shame is not like guilt. Guilt says, "I did something wrong," while shame says, "I am wrong." Guilt is the person who says, "I'm responsible, I messed up, I was wrong," and they expect punishment and need forgiveness. Shame is the person who thinks they don't belong because of something that they did or something that has been done to them.

Shame says you're not normal. You stick out and if people find out, you'll be kicked out.

Shame has no prejudices or preferences; it impacts each and every one of us. It doesn't matter who you are; it targets anyone and everyone.[11]

In *Soul Without Shame*, author Byron Brown suggests that we have a judge in our minds who presides over a courtroom of life. Living through our bodies and our energies, this judge is "a master of words, and yet you can feel it in your belly, your shoulders, and your jaw." Brown says, "Sometimes, you feel accused of doing something wrong or unthinkable; at other times, you feel you have been caught red-handed. Sometimes, you present a case for your own guilt and corruption; at other times, you argue hard to justify your innocence."[12]

Often our voices echo the judge—we reflect messages from the past. Whose voice do you hear with each self-judging statement within your mind? Perhaps the voice is yours now, but who said it first? Not you. It might have been a parent, a teacher, or a sibling. After hearing it enough, you began to believe it as truth. But it isn't. Your worth is *not* based on those types of statements.

I'm sure you've heard the word "corrosion." It's not a very positive word. We usually think of it in terms of a crumbling pipe or a deteriorating battery cable. The word actually means "to eat away, weaken, or destroy gradually."

Unfortunately, there are many who are raised in corrosive environments. The family may have been intact and finances stable, but the messages sent to the children were critical and toxic. They eventually began to erode what each child believed and how he or she felt about him- or herself. These messages gained a foothold and continued doing corrosive work for years. And the damage didn't have to occur with words. Often silence speaks louder than any voice.

We can't pronounce ourselves not guilty, but God can—and He does. Forgiveness is His work, His love, and His grace. He declares who and what we are. Isn't it better to have this come from Him than ourselves? Who is the most trustworthy? With God's help, the power of the past can be overcome.

Eliminating Guilt

We can learn to eliminate guilt. First of all, we'll identify where the beliefs we have about our anger came from and whether they're accurate or not. Often our beliefs and values come into play and generate the guilt we feel. Next, we'll make a list of the times when we either felt or expressed anger and what it was about. We'll determine whether our anger was justified or not for each case. Then we'll formulate a statement that we'll use next time the guilt occurs. Finally, we give ourselves permission to become angry when we need to.

What happens if we still feel guilty? We'll list three reasons for believing our anger is illegitimate and then three reasons for believing it is legitimate. Each day we'll give ourselves permission to feel anger, but when it occurs we won't express it outwardly. By making the choice not to express our anger, we're showing ourselves that we are in control. Feeling anger is okay—and nothing to feel guilty about. As we write down our thoughts, we'll also create a chart of our guilt levels for at least a month so we can track our progress.

The last step is to develop a positive plan in writing for how we'll express anger so moving forward we'll feel positive and in charge about its expression.

Expressing Anger

Jim was very direct as he discussed the way he expresses anger. "When I'm angry, you know it. So do the people who have upset me. I don't edit. I cut loose, and I don't care how they feel either. If they're hurt or put down, well, they deserved it after what they did or said to me. Sometimes other people in the same room feel my anger, but they could get out of the way."

Anger that hurts others is a problem. Too often anger attacks are misdirected at the other person's character rather than the actual action or lack of action. That's when anger is viewed as aggression and becomes a problem.

Tom told me of his anger pattern that had plagued him for years. "It's like I'm on an archery range. Every time I shoot at the target, I miss it and hit the target next to it. I was angry at my son the other day, and yet I took it out on my daughter. I guess I wasn't even aware that I was angry at him until I exploded. Then I had to deal with the problems my anger created between my daughter and me. This has happened at work as well. I'm often not aware that I'm angry with a coworker, and yet later on I'm griping my head off about him or her. I guess I was angry and took it out by griping."

At the present time, I too am periodically experiencing anger. It's not at anyone, but at the circumstances of what happened fairly recently. My remaining child, my daughter, died unexpectedly in her sleep. I'd planned to get together and talk over some issues. That opportunity is gone. There was much I wanted to say to her and to hear from her. Is there blame? Yes. Is there regret? Yes. Do I have anger? Yes—at myself and at the lost opportunity. How am I releasing this? Admission is the first step. I express my anger as I play the piano. Many of the piano selections lend themselves to the expression of feelings as my fingers strike the keys with force or a light, delicate touch. Sometimes I speak what my fingers are pouring into the keys. This is a healthy expression for me.

Crying is also a healthy expression of hurt that might turn into anger if left unresolved. Tears release a multitude of emotions. They stabilize the turmoil of our hearts and minds. The solvent of tears can bring balance to our emotions. On occasion, the tears may be few or they could be a torrent. I've experienced them rushing from my eyes like a flood, even during times when my thinking side wanted and tried to control their expression. Fortunately, over the years I've learned tears don't need to be restrained for they are gifts from God.

Tears have their own language. They even release chemicals that relax our nervous system and may point us to the reasons we need them. When words don't come or are insufficient, tears talk. We all need to cry. But for some, it's only allowed within. Hopefully, someday this moisture language will be available and visible to everyone, male and female. Crying often awakens what we've had difficulty discovering.

Crying is the cornerstone of grief, and lately it seems to be my constant companion. It is exhausting. Even as I write this, tears are forming. Do I know why? Not really, and I don't always have to know the specifics of the moment. Sometimes people see my tears and ask, "Is everything all right?" How do I answer? I hope with a "No, but thanks for asking. I'm doing okay." Tears release hurt; tears release sadness.

As I was writing this chapter, the loss of my daughter brought feelings and tears once more to the surface over the loss of my son, Matthew. He died in 1990 at the physical age of twenty-two. I found two written responses to my tears that I'd put in a grief folder. This first one I wrote nine months after Matthew's death:

January 5, 1991

Where have the tears gone? There was a time when I thought they would never end, but now I miss them as though they were a friend. There's only a mist where once a stream. The memories are fading all too fast, like it was last night's dream. It seems too soon to be this way, but I realize they may return yet another day. Who would have thought the sobs and clouded eyes would be missed, but they are. And yet, even as this is written, the words are difficult to see for some strange reason.

The poems and letters from friends help to bring back the loss again. Words of comfort expressed at the time of deepest pain help to keep Matthew's memory alive. For that's all we have of him now—memories. Someone else has the joy of his presence, his laugh, his smile, and his hugs.

Where have the tears gone? They haven't. They were hiding and waiting once again for the time to be called out to express the loss. They're here again, not as an intruder, but as a welcomed friend. Please don't stay away so long the next time. I need you. We need you.

In the fifteenth month, I wrote,

It's been some time since the feelings of grief came to the surface. You begin to wonder if they ever will again. But then they do. And each time is different. It began with finding some old pictures of Matthew when he was quite young, and in most of them he was smiling. Two days later we were watching Dr. Lloyd Ogilvie on a Sunday-morning TV program, and he read the passage in which the centurion came to Jesus about his son who was dying. Jesus told him to go home; his son would live. Both Joyce and I had the same response, "I wish that Jesus would have made that statement to us about Matthew." The tears came that morning. They will always be there and come when you least expect them. But they were there as part of our connection with something that we valued but lost, at least for the present time. They are also a reminder that our life is a series of transitions and changes, some of which we like and others we resist.

So, what we know is anger helps us release some of our *emotions*. And we need tears to release more of our emotions. One without the other is an incomplete release, and we may become stuck. If either one of these is stuck in our lives, we can ask God to work in our lives and help us discover and access each one. It's helpful and necessary to bring us out of the painful past to be fully in the present.

Establishing a Healthy Approach to Anger

Perhaps it will help us to think through what we want out of the role of anger in our lives. Once we have let those who hurt us off the hook, we can turn our focus on what we want to accomplish through the emotion of anger from this point forward. It sounds strange, doesn't it, to rationally decide what to do with anger? Consider these questions:

- What do you want to believe about anger?
- What do you want to feel about anger?
- How do you want to respond and react to the anger of others?
- How do you want to be free from the anger of others?
- How do you want to express your anger in positive, con-structive ways?

Answering these questions establishes our goal to become future thinkers. That's positive. We're developing and drawing toward a vision for our lives. When that happens, something dramatic will take place in our minds. We'll begin to think of the impossible as possible.

Remember the explorers and early pioneers? They believed there was something better out west. If we know Jesus Christ as Savior, we've been called to be pioneers—to think differently, believe differently, behave differently, and see life through a different lens of what can be rather than what was and is.

Someone has said that anger in a person indicates an unhealed hurt from the past. There will be times when the only way to get rid of anger and the desire for retribution will be to face the fact that we can't do anything to change what happened or prevent a similar occurrence in the future. Then we start the process of giving up a portion of our anger or resentment each day. One trauma victim said:

I finally realized that holding on to my anger kept me victimized. As much as I wanted someone to pay, I knew it wouldn't happen. So I decided on a 90-day plan. I would allow myself to keep 10 percent of my anger since I know I'm human and won't be perfect. But each day for 90 days, I would give up 1 percent of my anger. The fact that I had a goal and then developed a plan really encouraged my recovery. Each day I spent 15 to 20 minutes identifying who or what I wanted to avenge. I wrote it out each time and then put it in the form of a brief letter. I stood in a room and read it out loud unedited. Sometimes it wasn't pretty. And sometimes I read it to a friend because it helped having a live body there.

Each day I wrote the phrase, "I forgive you for…" and then put down the first reason I could think of for not forgiving. It was like I was full of rebuttals against forgiving. I would always end the morning by reading a praise psalm out loud. Then I thanked God for what He was doing, even if I was full of bitterness. It kept me pinned down and stuck. I didn't want to forgive. They didn't deserve it.

But I kept at it. I wondered after 30 days if I'd made even a 3-percent improvement. But by the time 60 days were over, I felt ahead of schedule. I was improving, I was growing. I got well. Sometimes the anger and grief still hit me. I can live with that even if it's a companion the rest of my life. I have days and weeks when I feel whole again. Praise God for this.

Taking positive steps like this will help us make the shift from victim to survivor. *Believing* that we can become survivors will accelerate this process.

Emotional Imprisonment and Debt

We are people who value freedom. There are numerous types of freedom, ranging from speech to how we worship. One of the freedoms that can cause tension and dismay when it's absent is *emotional freedom.* Many people feel restricted because of emotional debts. They are not emotionally free.

> To be emotionally free, you need to remove the obstacles that keep you in emotional debt. Emotional debt is any accumulation of unresolved old feelings that causes you to distort your view of the present. When you are in emotional debt, you consume so much energy trying to conceal old feelings that you have insufficient energy left to work effectively or to love with commitment. Unexpressed feelings also have great power to prejudice your judgment and over-sensitize you, causing you to take innocent events personally, overreact to them, lose control, and in so doing, lose faith in yourself.[13]

Emotional debt is when, due to an inability to face and resolve feelings as they occur, unresolved feelings are held inside. It's like wearing a suit of armor. We live with defensiveness that allows the present and future to be dictated or heavily influenced by the past.

> Unexpressed emotional obligations to past events demand expression in the present, often inappropriately. When you're emotionally indebted, you distort the present with your old emotional business. To free yourself from emotional debt, you must understand the meaning of your feelings and learn to express them directly.

> The third source of emotional debt is the result of failing to discover your gift. What is more painful than knowing you have not discovered and developed your talent, that you have missed your opportunity to make your mark on the world?

> Emotional freedom is being able to do what you want when you want to do it. Being emotionally free also means that you choose to do what is best for you because it pleases you to do so. When you're emotionally free, you believe in your own goodness and act to increase your worth. You

understand that whatever interferes with this belief is false, and you seek to exclude it.[14]

Emotional freedom means we're no longer held captive to our feelings, but we accept and use them in positive ways. We accept the way God created us emotionally. We benefit from our emotions and desire the best from them.

Chapter 5

Fear vs. Hope

I have some questions for everyone who struggles with emotions from the past. They're simple. They're basic. But they're very important:

- What fear controls your life?
- When is the last time you can remember being free from that fear?
- If you had the choice between hurting and healing, which would you choose?
- Are you thinking and behaving in ways that lead to healing or to hurt?

We might think everyone would choose healing. It makes sense. I know I would make that choice. Jesus asked a very similar question. He said to a sick man at a pool, "Do you want to get well?" The man had an excuse for why he was still lying by the pool waiting to get well (John 5:1-7). Many of us have similar excuses or reasons. This man had 38 years of opportunity. Somehow, during all that time, he couldn't find someone to help him into the pool within the time limitations. With people today, the reason is often fear—fear of the unknown and fear of being hurt...again.

All of us are afraid sometimes, which is normal. But some people are fearful most of the time and aren't necessarily aware of it. That's *not* normal. We weren't designed to be dominated by fear. We weren't created to dread life. If we're emotionally paralyzed, we end up refusing to participate in many of life's experiences. We consciously or unconsciously imprison ourselves.

Occasionally people tell me they're afraid of death. That's not unusual, but even more people I talk to are afraid of life in one way or another. Living life to its full potential is a threat to them. They're emotionally stuck and believe they can't successfully participate in many of life's activities and experiences. When counseling them, I often say, "It seems you're immobilized by fear." After some thought, they usually agree.

The fear of life is more debilitating than the fear of death. Fear disables. Fear shortens life. Fear cripples relationships. Fear hinders relationship with God. Fear makes life a daunting chore. Fear keeps us from experiencing the blessings of God because it short-circuits our choices and keeps us from growing through change. We have freedom in Christ, yet people often walk through life in a mobile prison of fear.

Fear can cause us to imagine the worst possible outcome of our efforts. Fear can limit the development of alternatives and put brakes on pursuing them. To protect ourselves from the disappointments that might occur if our efforts don't work out, we settle for less. Our dreams and hopes fade.

Fear also has a warning effect. It cautions us to be wary and hinders what we believe we can do to move ahead in positive ways. Unchecked fear destroys the reality of what might have been.[1]

Fear keeps us from saying, "I can," "I will," "I'm able," as well as "God is able." Whenever we give in to our fears, they grow larger, become more real, and finally keep us from being the dreamers and visionaries we were created to be.

Fear can turn us into yesterday people. Our resistance can keep us from experiencing the blessings God has for us. We are unable to focus our thoughts and beliefs so we can move forward. John Haggai said:

> Having a fear is like having a cancer. It is always there, hidden inside you, always sapping your strength and breaking your concentration. Even rational fear can be destructive in its effects. You cannot hide fear. Its destruction begins

by feeding on you, and then moving into your social and physical environment.[2]

There are at least two great motivating forces in life—fear and hope. Interestingly, both of these motivators can produce the same result. Fear is a powerful, negative drive.

Maureen was a woman living by fear. One day I asked her about her relationship with her mother. She said:

> Very distant. By choice, I live 1200 miles from my mother. When I call her she avoids significant conversation by talking about the weather. As one of nine children, I grew up struggling to find my own identity. I felt loved by my dad but not by my mom. In some ways, I got lost in the crowd.
>
> Actually there was no relationship with my mom. We lived in the same house, but that was it. She paid no attention to me. I was left to fend for myself as far back as I can remember. She was unmarried when I was born. I didn't fit in her plans…and never did. I felt like an accident. Taken from her at an early age, I was placed in a foster home. I was returned to her when she "proved" she could take care of me, but she didn't.
>
> She has always been a worrier, and I think some of that obsessiveness started to rub off on me when I graduated from college and got married. My sister and I have often talked about how we can feel like she is our mother, yet have no distinct emotional attachment to her. We both have vowed to be involved with our kids and to communicate with them and love them. I don't want her worries to become my children's worries.
>
> Because of Mom, I have trouble trusting myself and others. I'm often paralyzed by fear of failure and guilt over past failures. I suppress my emotions and my ability to hope, to dream about the future, and to set goals so I avoid failure and pain. I isolate myself emotionally from others. I

understand intellectually that I have worth, and I can see
that there are things I'm good at, but I still struggle to feel
like I'm worthy of good things, happiness, success, love.
Fears I learned from my mother are too real. They keep
me stuck.

Fear is also like a movie continually replaying our most haunting experiences. The message of fear movies is clear. Life is full of bad
experiences, and they will repeat themselves. An example of this is self-
sabotage. Those who live with fear often engage in acts that interfere
with their success or well-being.

Sabotage has a mission—to hinder, obstruct, waste, or destroy in
order to prevent success. It is carried out against enemies, usually sub-
tly and covertly. Sabotage happens in war when soldiers sneak behind
enemy lines to blow up bridges, interrupt supply lines, and disrupt
battle plans. It happens in politics when one candidate stoops to
rumor-starting, mudslinging, and character assassinations to discredit
opponents. It happens in sports when one racing team secretly tampers
with the engine of a rival team's car to gain an advantage.

Perhaps the most sinister and personally destructive act of sabotage is what people do to themselves. Some people are their own worst
enemy. They behave in ways that keep them from achieving goals and
joy. Usually they're not aware of what they're doing.

Often the root of this destructive behavior is a confusing and per-
plexing fear. This fear is very common today. I see it in the college
student who works hard during the semester and then inexplicably
chooses not to study for the final exam. I see it in the actor who fails to
show up for her final audition, even though she knows her lines per-
fectly and has succeeded in preliminary auditions. I see it in the exec-
utive who makes an unexplainable mistake in an area of his expertise,
and his mistake keeps him from the presidency of the company he's
served for twenty-three years.

I've been in classrooms where a student stopped cold in the middle of a presentation because of fear. The inability to cope can usually
be traced back to the amount of fear in their minds. That which they

feared the most had come upon them—and they made it happen by plunging unprepared into the scary situation.

Hope Provides Freedom

Hope is a totally different motivating force—a *positive* drive. Hope is like a magnet that draws us toward our goals. It expands our lives and brings beliefs of possibility and change for the better. It draws us away from the bad experiences of the past and pushes us toward better experiences in the future. The hope reel continually replays scenarios of potential successes. Hope causes us to say, "I can do it! I will succeed." Hope overrides "I don't feel safe."

We use the word "hope" so glibly. Have you ever said, "I hope it comes in the mail today," or "I hope I get that raise," or "I hope they're able to visit us this year"? Every time we use "hope" in this way, we're expressing a desire, but we are also wishing for something that is uncertain. We are using "hope" as a verb that usually refers to wishful thinking.

Sometimes we crank up our feelings to generate enough emotional or mental energy to bring something into reality. In a way we're saying, "I don't know for sure if this is going to happen. It might or might not, but I sure wish it would."

The Bible uses "hope" as a noun. "For most people, hoping is something that they *do*, but the Bible talks about hope as something they can possess."[3] Hope, in the Christian sense of the word, is far more than a wish or a dream. It's a tangible thing, as real as any object. "*We have this hope as an anchor for the soul, firm and secure*" (Hebrews 6:19). Our hope is a noun, as solid as a cast-iron anchor. And that hope is the hope of resurrection.[4]

In the Scriptures, hope is solid and sure. A certainty. There is no "maybe" or "I hope so" about it. "Hope is a person's eager expectation that something God has promised will certainly happen in the future." There's no question that God's promises will be kept.

> Hope is allowing God's Spirit to set us free and draw us forward.

Hope is not blind optimism: It's realistic optimism. People of hope are aware of the struggles and difficulties of life, but they live beyond them with a sense of potential, possibility, and expectation. A person of hope doesn't just live for the possibilities of tomorrow but also sees the possibilities of today even when it's not going well.

A person of hope doesn't just long for what's missing in life but also experiences what he or she has already received.

A person of hope can say an empathetic *no* to stagnation and an energetic *yes* to life.

Hope is allowing God's Spirit to set us free and draw us forward.

For the future to be different, we need to do something different.

> Paul said, "I press on toward the goal..." (Philippians 3:14). But what does it mean "to press"? Actually, it is a very important phrase that we use in many different ways. "To press" is to push as you push a button. "To press" is to exert pressure such as pressing or ironing clothes. "To press" is to make a great exertion as the weightlifter does when he "snatches" and "presses" several hundred pounds above his head. "To press" is to gamble, and it means go for broke. "To press" is to relentlessly pursue or intensely go after.[5]

"Press on." It's much better to be in the process of doing something than to be overwhelmed by discouragement. I've heard people say that having hope is a matter of personality type. Some people are born more hopeful than others. I don't believe that's true. *Hope is a choice,* an option. Many things happen in life over which we have no control, but we do have control over how we respond to them. When we have hope, some of the pain of a specific circumstance is eased because we're looking beyond this situation to what will happen in the future. Even if the situation can't be changed, our response to it can. We can choose to take charge rather than be victimized.

Powerful hope is not something we generate by ourselves. It happens because our focus is on God—who He is and how He perceives us. Hope increases as we move ahead. When we take our eyes off Christ, hope can erode. When hope erodes, it causes us to give up, fold, cave in, or live with resignation. Sometimes the emotion of hope is like an avalanche that is over in twenty seconds. A negative experience hits us hard, and hope suddenly goes flat. At other times, hope may erode so gradually that we're not even aware of it until we realize we're just going through life with no ambition and not feeling blessed.

> The loss of hope is not simply pessimism about the future, it is a sense of abandonment and loss of connections in the present. Only the pain is real and it feels like it will go on forever; the dust of its ashes hangs in the air and damages the ability to breathe.
>
> The hurt or trauma we've experienced disrupts and ruptures our previous understanding of life. Our journey toward healing requires a new vision that both knows the depth of the wound and has witnessed the possibility for hope.[6]

This is why hope is so important.

I see hopeless-feeling people in my office every week. There are so many times when I wish I could reach out and give these people physical hope. We can become so despondent and discouraged that we must rely on the hope of others to carry us along until our own hope returns or develops. Hopelessness is at the core of depression.

The good news is that hope can grow. Often it means not letting our situation or circumstance control us. When we're discouraged and hurt, God is still alive and still loves us even if we aren't feeling His love momentarily.

Tackling Fear

"The best way to begin overcoming a fear is to face it a little at a time and from a safe distance."[7] Fear is a reality in all our lives. And if hurt has been a major struggle, we may deal with fear frequently. Fear of the unknown is part of taking a risk. We tend to stick to what we know, whether good or bad, because we find comfort and safety in the familiar.

The most difficult fears to recognize are those associated with people and social functions. These include rejection, anger, disapproval, failure, and, yes, success. There are two primary reasons these fears are difficult to identify. First, many people recognize the presence of fear but devote their efforts to justifying it as a reasonable, legitimate emotion. Second, the fear of people is difficult to spot because those who suffer from it strategically avoid situations where it might surface.

There's another group who may not be afraid of their feelings, but they are afraid of their thoughts. Most of us have wished that a frightening thought would go away—or would never have entered our minds in the first place. Occasional thoughts like these are normal and relatively harmless, but the persistent fear of trauma is something to be concerned about.

Let's consider two important steps in moving on from the past. How can we address our fears so they no longer control us?

The first step is admitting and identifying our fears. The best way is taking the time to identify each fear and asking God to help us bring our fears to the surface so we can face them. Fill in this statement several times:

- What I do or don't do because of my fear is...
- What I do or don't do because of my fear is...
- What I do or don't do because of my fear is...
- What I do or don't do because of my fear is...
- What I do or don't do because of my fear is...

> As you begin to overcome your fears, be realistic about your expectations. If you were to chart your improvement on a graph, don't expect to see a straight, upward line of uninterrupted success. Your growth and improvement will come in a series of ups and downs, and there will be times when your fears are actually worse.[8]

We need to anticipate and plan for the down times. If we don't, we'll be thrown by the apparent reversal in our progress. We'll be tempted to think we haven't made any improvement at all, which isn't true. What we choose to focus on in those down moments will affect our attitude for the next several days.

If we're coming to grips with a longstanding fear we haven't confronted for years, things might get worse *at first*. Face the fear and resist the sense of failure.

Why don't more people try the gradual approach to facing their fears? They're often too busy avoiding the object or situation that frightens them to take a steady step-by-step approach. And when they do decide to tackle the problem, they think they can lick it immediately once and for all.

The next step is facing the two fears we've mentioned—if we are afraid of the unknown, identify what we're afraid of. Be specific. Perhaps we can identify with Terry. He told me:

> I want certainty in my life. I don't want any surprises. The unknown is scary. What if I can't deal with what comes? What if it's more than I can handle or it's worse than anything I've ever experienced? What if it takes away what security I have? I don't need any more pain in my life.

Most of us live with a series of what ifs. What can we do? Take each fear and reverse it. For example, if we say, "What if I can't handle what comes?" and then reverse it to "What if I can handle it?" If we say, "What if it takes away my security?" and then reverse it to "What if it helps me feel more secure?" Change our statements. Take charge!

Write each of the following Scriptures on separate index cards. When we're struggling with the fear of the unknown or the hurt, we can read each one out loud and envision ourselves applying each truth to our lives.

> So do not fear, for I am with you; do not be dismayed, for I am your God. I will strengthen you and help you; I will uphold you with my righteous right hand (Isaiah 41:10).

> When you pass through the waters, I will be with you; and when you pass through the rivers, they will not sweep over you. When you walk through the fire, you will not be burned; the flames will not set you ablaze (Isaiah 43:2).

> Anxiety weighs down the heart, but a kind word cheers it up (Proverbs 12:25).

> All the days of the afflicted are bad, but a glad heart has a

continual feast [regardless of the circumstances] (Proverbs 15:15 AMP, brackets in original).

Don't worry about anything; instead, pray about everything. Tell God what you need, and thank him for all he has done. Then you will experience God's peace, which exceeds anything we can understand. His peace will guard your hearts and minds as you live in Christ Jesus. And now, dear brothers and sisters, one final thing. Fix your thoughts on what is true, and honorable, and right, and pure, and lovely, and admirable. Think about things that are excellent and worthy of praise. Keep putting into practice all you learned and received from me—everything you heard from me and saw me doing. Then the God of peace will be with you (Philippians 4:6-9 NLT).

Taming the "what if" monster can often take a deeper examination of each one. If the worst we can imagine were to happen, what would that mean? In what ways would our lives go on or not go on? What would we do? What would our lives be like, and what would we do to keep hope alive? We need to know there is life at the other end of our fears, even our greatest ones.[9] (For more ideas and resources on developing a new path and pattern of thinking, check out my book *A Better Way to Think*.)

If our choice is that of healing our past, let's think of "who" and "what" *we* want to be. This is our journey, and it's important we choose our destination. Many individuals create a vision of this destination by first asking, "Who do I want to become?"

Another question to ask is, "Where would I rather be in my life right now?" Some people may say they don't want to be who they are, be on the path they're on, and be stuck in the past. But that is only part of the journey. Instead of dwelling on the past, we need to look forward to see where we are going and discover ways for moving forward. The more time and effort we invest, the more results we'll experience. Whatever we decide, it is vital to handwrite our questions and answers. This may seem strange in this day and age, but writing (not inputting) our thoughts reinforces them in our brains. So let's put our computers away, as well as any other texting gadget. Handwriting helps the brain that has been disrupted in its functioning because of trauma to operate as it should. The other process that is important is to *say aloud what we plan on doing*. This way the new information and plans will reach our brains in a visual manner and in auditory form. Between the two, our brains accept this new information that can override the old memories and lessen the impact of the past.

This is how we turn from fear to hope. Remember that God's gift is grace—and this grace overcame the past and gave us a future. We do have a choice in life—to live driven by fear or to be drawn forward by hope. Frederick Buechner wrote:

> Hope stands up to its knees in the past and keeps its eyes on the future. There has never been a time past when God wasn't with us as the strength beyond our strength, the wisdom beyond our wisdom, as whatever it is our hearts…that keeps us human enough at least to get by despite everything in our lives that tends to wither the heart and make us less than human. To remember the past is to see that we are here today by grace…[10]

Chapter 6

Our Brain

I t weighs approximately three pounds, regardless of our body weight. It makes our heart beat, our lungs breathe, and our limbs mobilize. This unique mass directs what we do. It's amazing in what it does, a mystery in how it does it, and a wonder because it's home to our mind. It changes every minute of every day. Over 90 percent of what we know about it has been discovered in the last ten years. It's involved in all we experience, including our past and present.[1]

Yes, it's our brain.

We were created in such a marvelous way, especially our brains. Perhaps this biblical verse describes it best: "I praise you because I am fearfully and wonderfully made; your works are wonderful, I know that full well" (Psalm 139:14).

Our brains have two distinct parts. First of all, we have bilingual brains. It's true. The left side of our brain speaks one language, and the right side speaks another. The right side is the emotional side. It is intuitive, visual, and spatial. This side carries the music of experience. It stores the memories of the senses, such as sounds, touch, and smell. It's full of pictures that run like a silent movie.

When we were being carried in our mothers' wombs, the right side of our brains developed first. This side carries the nonverbal communication between mother and child. When we communicate using this side, we use facial expressions and body language, as well as singing, swearing, crying, and so forth.

Our left side of the brain is the chatterbox. It controls all the talking.

It remembers facts, statistics, and the vocabulary of events. It's full of words and narration. It's the seat of logic. But for this side to describe, tell a story, or share an autobiographical narration, it needs to reach over to the right side and draw on the emotional memories stored there. That's what *should* happen. But here's the problem for those who are traumatized. The left and right sides don't get together that well. The growth of the connection between the two sides has been hampered.[2]

The worst experience for a young child is neglect because it affects every part of the developing neurological system. When children are born, the neurons in their brains are waiting to be stimulated and put into use. This promotes growth that expands their capacities to understand the world. Lack of stimulation can lead to atrophy in the neurons. Lack of stimulation also affects the size and strength of the neural networks within the brain. The brains of neglected children, including those who were physically, emotionally, and sexually traumatized, have been found to be smaller in overall size. Research indicates that chronic childhood abuse causes different and more intense changes in a person than a negative event that occurs in adulthood. It takes longer to overcome the impact of childhood abuse.[3] A child becomes stuck emotionally at the age when he or she was abused. This is why a ten- or twelve-year-old child may behave like a five-year-old.

Traumatized people have alterations in their brains. Memory is affected, which often creates lapses and deficits in verbal ability and short-term memory. Imaging scans clearly show that past trauma activates the right hemisphere of the brain and deactivates the left.[4] Trauma is intrusive and invasive. It interrupts and derails us. It can constrict and limit our lives significantly. Sometimes we alternate between the two sides of the brain. We find ourselves caught between amnesia and reliving the trauma; between floods of intense feeling and arid states of no feelings whatsoever; between irritable impulsive action and complete inhibition of action.[5]

After trauma, we experience the world with a different nervous system. The survivor's energy becomes focused on suppressing inner chaos at the expense of spontaneous involvement in life.[6] One of the many paradoxes of trauma damage occurs when we remember too much, and yet damage also occurs when we remember too little.[7]

A Quick Inventory

Indicate what you've experienced.

• Amnesia	Yes	No	Maybe
• Impulsive and risky actions	Yes	No	Maybe
• Intense feelings	Yes	No	Maybe
• No action/immobilized	Yes	No	Maybe
• No feelings/numbness	Yes	No	Maybe
• Reliving traumatic experiences such as flashbacks or intrusive thoughts.	Yes	No	Maybe

When something happens that reminds a traumatized person of the past, that person's right brain reacts as if the traumatic event were happening in the present. Overload often occurs, and the ability of this side of the brain is decreased; therefore, the brain is less able to do left-brain functions. It can't distinguish a real threat from a false threat. The section of the brain that is supposed to analyze isn't working well. It limits the person in how to put into words what he or she is feeling.

Because the analysis process is impaired, people may not be aware they are reexperiencing and reenacting the past. They just know they are furious, terrorized, enraged, ashamed, or frozen. When words fail, haunting images capture the experience and return as nightmares and flashbacks from the right side of the brain.

The right side, which is the alarm section, reacts *too much*. We're activated to face danger when there isn't any. It's like a car alarm system that keeps going off even when no one has touched the vehicle. The owner with the key isn't around to turn it off, so the chaos continues. Brain scans of trauma victims reliving the experience show a lot of lighting up on the right side and very little on the left, which implies that people aren't thinking as much with the left side of their brains.[8] After the emotional storm passes, the person may look for somebody or something to blame for setting them off.

Male and Female Differences

We know there are differences between the male and female brains. In general, men tend to have larger brains. Women have greater density in the language areas, the decision-making portions, and the memory portion. Female emotional circuitry reaction is often larger as well.

There is a connector between the two sides of the brain, which is how the two sides communicate. It's a series of nerve bundles that brings together the emotional and thinking sides of our existence. Women have up to 40 percent more of these nerve bundles than men, which means women are better able to use both sides of their brain at the same time. Men have to switch from one side of the brain to the other, depending on what they need in the situation. Women enjoy more cross talk between sides of the brain. This is why women can usually handle several tasks at one time and develop reading skills earlier than males.

Understanding Brain Function

Humans need the functions of both sides of the brain to have balance and to derive the most out of life. To better understand how the brain works without getting into medical jargon, Bessel van der Kolk uses these practical, easy-to-remember names for some of the sections of the brain: the Cook, the Smoke Detector, and the Watch Tower.[9]

Imagine that over the years we've eaten homemade split-pea soup regularly. It contains peas and numerous other items. We could eat the various ingredients by themselves—ham, peas, carrots, onions—and say we've had split-pea soup, but the reality is we didn't since the only way and the best way it could be split-pea soup is to have everything blended together. "The Cook" makes the soup come alive.

The Cook takes all the perceptions that impact the brain and stirs them up into a blended autobiographical soup called "This is what's happening to me." (The Cook's true name is "the thalamus.")

The Cook controls the senses. It receives incoming information through our senses of sight, smell, hearing, touch, and taste, and then passes them on to the other part of the brain responsible for processing. It relays information to the portion where memories are stored and activates related memories. If a negative memory is activated and alerted, the emotional response carried back to the Cook will also be a negative feeling.

At this point, the information is passed on in two different directions—one is to a couple of small glands we'll call the Smoke Detector and the other is to the frontal lobes or the Watch Tower, the conscious part of our brains. The Smoke Detector takes the incoming information and identifies whether the information is relevant for survival. If it senses a threat, the Smoke Detector sends out an instant message to prepare us to handle it. We're put on alert.

Dogs can be a good illustration of this. The number of dog breeds is huge. Some are bred to herd other animals. Some assist in hunting by flushing out prey or pointing. Some are used for heavy labor, such as huskies pulling hundreds of pounds of goods on sleds. Still others use their heightened sense of smell for searching out drugs, dead bodies, and cancer. The Smoke Detector is like a dog—but unlike any just mentioned. It's a watchdog that's constantly on duty. Some people live as though they're on permanent alert. They are hypervigilant.

The Smoke Detector is also the site of emotional memory. It's the centerpiece of our emotional system. This memory system is very refined. It records memories of any traumas we've experienced. It stores sights, smells, and sounds of our worst experiences. It's not in the rational department, so don't expect logic. The Smoke Detector matches what is being experienced now with what has occurred in the past, but because it doesn't operate on reason or logic, it doesn't care whether the responses make sense or not. When we reexperience what we've already gone through, it's because the watchdog part of our brain went into action.[10]

At night we rest, but this portion of the brain continues to monitor sensory information for any sign of threat. If there's an earthquake, or a door slams shut, or the cat knocks a vase to the floor, it detects the menacing noise and instantly activates its connections to the startle response so we leap out of bed—heart racing—ready to protect ourselves.[11] It also becomes highly active when we're remembering a traumatic incident. It controls our behavior. When we've been in trauma, the Smoke Detector becomes hypersensitive and overreacts to normal stimuli.

The Smoke Detector is concerned with our survival. It's dependent on another portion of the brain for feedback as well as preparing the body to handle the threat. Personally, I call this aspect the Smoke Detector's Assistant.

The Assistant is connected to long-term memory storage and locates events in time and place. That's one of its biggest jobs. For example, when fear comes, it remembers where we were and what we were doing at the time. It's responsible for writing the story of the trauma, and it updates memory with any new information. This is the portion of the brain that calms us down. It's also highly affected by ongoing trauma and can actually shrink in size.

This emotional system doesn't allow us to think about our reactions. That takes too much time. And it doesn't care if it makes us miserable. Under extreme stress, it shuts down the thinking part of our brain.[12]

The Smoke Detector triggers the mind and the body to prepare for action. When the danger is past, it returns to its normal state. These two little alarm glands are fairly good at picking up danger clues for us to access when we've experienced trauma.[13]

Then there is the third section, the Watch Tower. Its real name is the "prefrontal cortex," and it's located right above our eyes. The front part of our brain makes assessments. If the Smoke Detector alerts us and it's a false alarm, the Watch Tower lets us know it's a false alarm so our stress level can go down. This brain section helps us observe what is happening, predict what will happen depending on various factors, and allows us to make conscious choices. It acts as the *supervisory system* for the emotional side and the thinking side of the brain. It could be called the *supervisor,* but strong emotions can shut it down.[14] As long as this portion of our brain is working as it should, we'll have the balance we want and the ability to handle stress. People who have posttraumatic stress disorder have a difficult time with this balance, and they have difficulty controlling their emotions and impulses. When survival is at stake, we usually stop listening to voices of reason. Arguing with a person in survival mode seldom is effective.

Emotions and the Brain

We are emotional creations. God created us and how we function. And the most amazing and perhaps least understood part of us is our brain. We may think, "I'm not influenced by my emotions that much. I'm a thinking, rational being." That may be true, but our brain and mind are created in such a way that no information gets through to the rational thinking part without passing through the area of the brain where emotions originate. Emotions color that information and also determine how much attention is paid to it, whether we consciously acknowledge it or not.

When our emotional side (the right side of the brain) is highly activated, we tend to shut down the thinking or rational left side. It's like we're caught in an emotional grip or vise, but we insist that our thinking, even though highly influenced by our emotions, is accurate and logical, whereas in reality it might not be. Someone described this like his emotions hijacked the rational side of his brain. No matter how much insight and understanding we develop, our rational, left side of the brain is basically impotent to talk the emotional right brain out of its own reality.[15]

Has anyone ever said to you, "Quit responding with your emotions. Just think about this, and you'll respond better as well as calm down?" Does this work? No it doesn't, and it won't.

Based on our life experiences, we may develop an "emotional allergy," which is an intense reactivity to a situation that is similar to an event that was painful in the past, but it is *not* the same situation in the present. It's as if one hint in the present that brings up the past is the same as the past—even when our present situation is quite different.

Remember these three portions of your brain—the Cook, the Smoke Detector and its Assistant, and the Watch Tower. There are other sections, but for our purpose these will be important to remember. What happens inside us due to past events will be reflected in these sections of our brains.

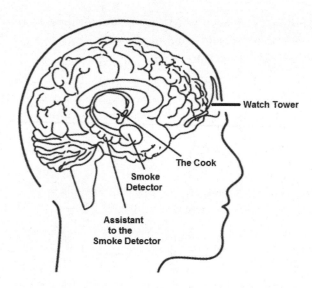

Figure 1: Four parts of the brain important in dealing with past trauma

Trauma Impacts the Brain

We've discussed trauma, but let's briefly consider how it impacts our brain. It is as though trauma causes the left side (the cognitive or thinking side) and the right side (the emotional) to become disconnected from one another. Usually our body, emotions, and thoughts are all connected, but trauma separates them.

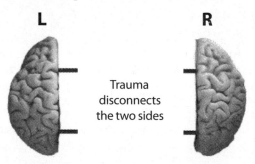

Figure 2: Trauma disconnects our emotions and logic

The left brain and right brain have to pull together, otherwise just one side is in charge. We may have vivid, graphic thoughts about what happened but no emotion. Or we may experience intense emotions without the thoughts or actual memories. As one man said, "I felt like my brain was disrupted, and one part transmitted on AM and the other on FM. Sometimes there are holes in my memory, like a slice was taken out. Other times I can't get those intrusive, unwanted memories to stop. I want them evicted! I can't remember what I want to remember, and I can't forget what I want erased." This struggle is shared by many.[16]

Think of the mind or brain as a bank. Like most banks, we can make deposits and withdrawals. Sometimes it's best to make a deposit, but there are times it's best to make a withdrawal. My parents opened a savings account for me when I was two or three. I never made a deposit myself; my parents took care of that for me. And because they made wise choices, the money they put in for me grew over the years. What they did was for my benefit, and the results were positive. At the proper time, we withdrew the money and put it to good use.

In our bank accounts, other people make deposits along with us. Sometimes our deposits earn money, but depending on the economy we could lose money. We might earn more by investing it elsewhere. Some of the deposits to our minds should never have been made. They were based on distortion, misinformation, and even fear. When we discover we've made a bad investment at a bank, the wise step is to immediately make a withdrawal. But too many hang on to what was deposited (their past), fail to check how it is doing, and so end up losing money. Negative statements that were made, as well as any form of abuse, are destructive deposits that, if left unchecked, grow and interfere with the present. How we think and respond to others is directly related to the thoughts deposited in our memory banks. *We can only draw on what has been deposited.* It may be time to make some withdrawals so we can start living freely today.

> The solution [is] to give God control.

We have no control over deposits made in our minds when we were children, but as adults we do. It's time to clear out the account in your bank and make new, healthy deposits. We want our brains to function the way God intended.

People sometimes ask, "Is it possible to get a brain or mind transplant?" We all laugh…at first…but the idea isn't without appeal. It sometimes feels like it would be easier to start over with a clean slate rather than to continue enduring the turmoil that occurs inside our minds or go through all the work it takes to change entrenched patterns. The good news is that according to Scripture, it is possible to change our minds. The Bible records that "the LORD saw how great the wickedness of the human race had become on the earth, and that *every inclination of the thoughts of the human heart was* only evil all the time" (Genesis 6:5). Isn't it interesting that the first place human beings turned away from God was through their thoughts?

Centuries later, the apostle Paul was still stating the same problem. "Although they knew God, they neither glorified him as God nor gave thanks to him, but *their thinking became futile and their foolish hearts were darkened*" (Romans 1:21). Wrong thinking can develop from what impacted us in the past.

The solution isn't to try to control the content of our minds on our own. Instead, we need to choose to give God control. Romans 8:5-7 warns:

> Those who live according to the flesh have their minds set on what the flesh desires; but those who live in accordance with the Spirit have their minds set on what the Spirit desires. The mind governed by the flesh is death, but the mind governed by the Spirit is life and peace. The mind governed by the flesh is hostile to God; it does not submit to God's law, nor can it do so.

Our goal should be to let our minds be controlled by the Holy Spirit. We want to set our minds on what God wants. Here's the good news: *What we think can be reversed!* Like a boat that's been moving in the wrong direction, we can turn our thinking around and start moving our lives in another direction. (For additional information, read my book *A Better Way to Think*, Baker Books, 2011.)

We've all struggled to change our thought life. We've tried different approaches or programs, prayed, been prayed over, and so on. But we still struggle. Any change we want to make is not a simple step-by-step process or an overnight event. That's because our brains weren't designed to make sudden and permanent changes. The brain follows patterns of habits established over the years. We can't expect this unique organ of the body—with its billions of neurons and millions of pathways, circuits, and memory cells—to erase what it has built over years and replace it with entirely new thinking instantaneously. So, when we begin changing old patterns, we need to expect our old ways of thinking and talking to challenge the new. We're likely to tell ourselves, "This won't work." We don't believe the new thoughts. We've disrupted the old way of thinking, and now we're trying to resist the new. God's Word says:

> Do not be conformed to this world [any longer with its superficial values and customs], but be transformed and progressively changed [as you mature spiritually] by the renewing of your mind [focusing on godly values and ethical attitudes], so that you may prove [for yourselves] what the will of God is, that which is good and acceptable and perfect [in His plan and purpose for you] (Romans 12:2 AMP, brackets in original).

The "renewing of your mind" in this verse refers to the spirit of the mind. Under the controlling power of the Holy Spirit, we believers can direct our thoughts and energies toward God. The renewing of the mind is the adjustments to our thinking and outlook on life so they conform to the mind of God. We want our minds to be focused on Christlike thoughts, as we're instructed in Colossians 3:1-2: "Since, then, you have been raised with Christ, set your hearts on things above, where Christ is, seated at the right hand of God. Set your minds on things above, not on earthly things." The phrase "set your hearts on" means "to think on" or "focus on." Ephesians 1:18 speaks of having the eyes of our heart enlightened. The Amplified Version says having the eyes of our heart flooded with light by the Holy Spirit. Ephesians 4:22-23 (AMP) admonishes: "Put off your old self [completely discard your former nature], which is being corrupted through deceitful desires, and be continually renewed in the spirit of your mind [having a fresh, untarnished mental and spiritual attitude]."

Our brain's ability to change was greatest in childhood and adolescence. Don't be discouraged if it takes a little longer now. Brainpower does not decrease with age, so knowledge, intelligence, and abilities can be acquired later in life. Scientists have discovered that the brain has the ability to add new nerve cells, change the way different regions communicate, and even rewire or replace some of its parts, remapping message pathways. This can occur, to some degree, throughout our lives.[17] This is so important for the healing of our past.

For thinking to change, we need a new vision, a new goal. It involves identifying the way we want our thinking to be. We create a new pattern of thinking and a new way of self-communication. But it's more than that. In *Living Above the Level of Mediocrity,* Chuck Swindoll describes what developing a vision entails:

> Vision is the ability to see God's presence, to perceive God's power, to focus on God's plan, in spite of the obstacles… Vision is the ability to see above and beyond the majority. Vision is perception—reading the presence and power of God into one's circumstances. I sometimes think of vision as looking at life through the lens of God's eyes, seeing situations as He sees them. Too often we see things not as they are, but as we are. Think about that. Vision has to do with looking at life with a divine perspective, reading the scene with God in clear focus.
>
> Whoever wants to live differently in "the system" must correct his or her vision.[18]

There is so much to learn about the functioning of our brains. For example, in our brains, circuits and neutrons are primary in improving brain functioning. This occurs by continuing to learn. Here are a few more facts about your brain and mine.

- Exercise is critical throughout our lifetime for better brain functioning. For example, a daily one-mile walk reduces dementia risk by 50 percent.

- Your brain thrives on words either spoken or thought about. The more words we use, the better it is for our brains.

- In terms of focused attention, multitasking is detrimental.

- The more we learn, the more we'll grow and change.

To enhance the health of your brain, read *Optimizing Brain Fitness* by Richard Restak (The Great Courses, 2011).

We don't have to take these steps by ourselves because humans are limited. God is not. We can ask Him to change us from the inside out. Let's take our thoughts and our pasts to Him. We are never alone.

Chapter 7

Grieving Past Losses

Losses in life abound. We're aware of some of them, while others are hidden. Most losses deliver pain, which we accept, but there are other aspects to pain that can increase it substantially. Losses come in many forms and packages. Some things and experiences are just that. Something is gone, missing, a hole in our life. Losses also occur because something was added. This could be by choice or not.

Many people believe loss is something we need to get over as soon as possible. Any loss is a disruption in our lives. Some will alter the shape and outlook of our lives.

- Loss is not meant to be delayed, but often it is; thus, the pain is intensified.

- Loss is not meant to be unresolved, but when this occurs the original pain intensifies.

- Loss is not meant to cripple, but when it does the loss becomes paralyzing.

- Loss, unfortunately, comes in many forms with lingering results.

Once again we're dealing with buried grief. If we were mistreated or abused, we learned to adapt to survive, but it cost us. We buried the grief that was difficult to work through. We may acknowledge our losses, but we can't count on others to do the same. We might not be recognized as someone with "legitimate" grief by some. Maltreatment may be the reason for being stuck in the past. When we can't or don't respond emotionally in a healthy way, we create a platform for additional losses.

We need to recognize and identify every loss in our lives so we can grieve, just as we do if someone died. For several years, I've been asking my counselees, "What losses have you experienced that you never fully grieved for?" Most of them, either immediately or within two or three weeks, are able to recognize some losses they'd previously failed to view that way and, therefore, had failed to grieve.

When we don't grieve properly, unresolved reactions and feelings lead to a higher level of discomfort. This pain prevents us from living life to the fullest. Let's consider what many individuals lose and whether these could be some of your losses as well.

- Many lose a sense of safety and security in their world.
- Many lose or fail to develop the ability to mourn.
- Many experience a loss of the sense of wholeness. They feel fragmented.
- Many find it difficult to develop and maintain healthy relationships—the feeling of attachment to others is missing, or trusting is difficult, or just determining where they fit is a problem.

Early childhood losses can predispose us to oversensitivity and depression because we compound our losses. We pile one loss on top of another. Instead of experiencing one at a time and dealing with the grief of that loss, we just move on. Consequently, each loss or problem appears to be larger than it actually is. It's fairly common to compound losses, but when that happens, we must unpack them, separate them, and focus our thinking on them one by one.[1]

One of the most damaging losses of life is abandonment. Some children are physically abandoned, but this number is far surpassed by those who have been emotionally abandoned. They know their parents never leave them alone and their physical needs are met, but their emotional needs are neglected. There is no nurturing, hugging, or healthy intimacy. The verbal affirmations children so desperately need are shrouded in silence. Soon the children begin to wonder, *What is wrong with me?* This perception is carried with them into their adult lives.

Over the years to help people understand their pasts and be able to move on, I've asked some simple, clarifying questions. Often as they share the answers, the reasons for where they are today become apparent. I remember asking Vicki, "How would you describe your relationship with your father?" She said:

> He was controlling, a perfectionist, military man, and unfortunately, an alcoholic. I was fearful of him, yet wanting to have his approval and love. My sister, mother, and I were all afraid of him. For example, he would come up to my room with white gloves on and check for dust and then try to bounce a quarter off my bed. I can laugh about it now, but back then we lived waiting for the other shoe to drop. My father was sexually abusive with me as well. It is difficult to put into words the ambivalence I felt toward him. I loved him yet hated what he was doing to me.

I said, "Parents influence our lives in many ways. In spite of how you described him, will you describe how your father has influenced or shaped your life negatively or positively?" Vicki replied,

> Negative: I had no concept of healthy boundaries; therefore, relationships were unhealthy (I didn't know where I stopped and others began). Only by the grace of God, my husband and I have been married twenty-eight years. Spiritually, I struggled in believing in God because my father was a Sunday-school teacher and deacon in our church. Emotionally, I was fragile. I had to work hard to overcome many fears throughout my life. I was filled with constant worry, always on the alert, waiting for the other shoe to drop. I know now that even my brain was affected due to the trauma. Through many years of Christian counseling, God has paved new pathways in my brain rather than have me remain stuck in fear and insecurity. And intimacy was

something else that needed to receive the healing touch of God.

I think the only way my dad influenced me positively is I have put the negative into the hands of God, and I constantly asked Him how to turn this around to good. God has taught me how to work hard to find who I am in Him. I believe to the depths of my heart that God is my Father, and I am adopted by Him. God has also put many positive, fatherly men in my life. It has taken me a long time to trust them, but they have shaped me in many positive ways. But it takes so long…

When I heard Vicki say, "God has paved new pathways in my brain," I was amazed at her insight. That is exactly what had to happen and why there is so much said in this book about that aspect of brain recovery.

The death of either parent is also a devastating loss for a child. For many, the sadness they carry about in adulthood can be traced to the childhood loss of their father. With children, their limited capability to process a death cognitively, as well as grieve properly, means they usually regrieve at major developmental times of their lives. And the loss can come back with intensity. One woman shared with me this poem she wrote:

> And you asked where he went
> And they said:
> Heaven.
> And they took you to a field of tombstones and Columbine.
> They said
> This is where his perfect body lay.
> And you were confused.
> Now there was two of him
> And none of you.[2]

Time and time again, I've seen the losses not grieved in childhood interfere with an adult's way of responding to life and marriage. The type and number of losses a child experiences are too many to identify here. In this book, our main concerns are what can be done about damaging losses in childhood and is recovery possible.

Once again there are times when we lose hope and remain stuck with pain from the past. Have you ever caught some flies and imprisoned them in a glass jar with air holes at the top? Some of us did this as children. The flies buzzed around frantically looking for a way out of the jar. But if we kept the jar closed for several days something interesting happened. When we took the perforated lid off, the flies didn't try to escape. Even though there was no lid, the creatures were so used to flying around in a circle, they continued to do so. And even when they got close to the top, they went right back to flying around in circles.

Sometimes we do the same thing. We carry our losses with us like emotional baggage, and even though the lid of the jar has been removed, we continue to fly in circles. If we were wounded by losses in childhood, we developed a tendency toward depression. For some, there is a prevailing sense of sadness that lingers just beneath the surface. Occasional journeys into this realm are normal and give depth of balance to our lives. Sadness can cause us to become more contemplative, serious, thoughtful, and grateful. It can give us new purpose for living life to the fullest. However, constant sadness takes the sunshine and delight out of life.

Our losses are going to change our values. The questions "Why did I spend so much time on that?" and "Why did I waste all those years?" are common when someone is grieving over the loss of a loved one. Hopefully we learn through these experiences to the extent that our lives are different.[3]

With any loss, grief tries to take over. When grief is our companion, we experience it psychologically through our feelings, thoughts, and attitudes. It impacts us socially as we interact with others. Our experience is also physical. Sadness affects our health and is expressed in bodily symptoms. Our body grieves and our mind grieves.

Grief flits in and out of our lives. It is a natural, normal, predictable, and expected reaction to loss. As hard as it can be, grieving is normal. The *absence* of grief is abnormal. Grief is a personal experience. Loss does not have to be accepted or validated by others for us to know, experience, and express grief.[4] A hopeful scripture that reflects on this is Psalm 73:26 (NLT): "My health may fail, and my spirit may grow weak, but God remains the strength of my heart; he is mine forever."

Why do we have to go through this experience of grief? What is the purpose? Grief responses express three basic things:

- Through grief we express our feelings of our loss.

- Through grief we express our protest at the loss, as well as our desire to change what happened and have it not be true.

- Through grief we express the effects we have experienced from the devastating impact of the loss.[5]

The purpose of grieving over loss is to get beyond these reactions to face the loss and work toward adapting to the changes. The overall point of grief is to bring us to the point of making necessary changes so we can live with the loss in a healthy way. We start with "Why did this happen to me?" Eventually we move on to "How can I learn through this experience? How can I go on with my life?" When the "how" question replaces the "why" question, we have started to adapt to the reality of the loss. "Why" questions reflect a search for meaning and purpose in loss. "How" questions reflect searching for ways to adjust to the loss.[6]

Despite all our questioning, perhaps there simply aren't any answers to the why questions. Maybe we *don't* know why and we *can't* know why. Maybe that's all we know. As one survivor wrote,

I don't know why.
I'll never know why.
I don't have to know why.
I don't like it.
What I have to do is make a choice about my living.[7]

Our goal is to be able to say:

This loss I've experienced is a crucial upset in my life. In fact, it is the worst thing that will ever happen to me. But

is it the end of my life? No. I can still have a rich and fulfilling life. Grief has been my companion and has taught
me much. I can use it to grow into a stronger person than
I was before my loss.[8]

Grief is a required task in breaking free from the past and learning to live in the present. For many, the losses during childhood keep
them stuck. These traumas need to be faced and revealed. Why should
we spend time grieving something from so long ago? Grieving will
help us work through the death-like experiences of being trapped in
the emotions or trauma of the past. Far too often, as children, we take
the blame and responsibility for what we experienced, and this is just
not true.[9]

There were people in our past who were not who we thought they
were, nor were they who they should have been.

- We needed them to be supportive, and they were not.
  That's a loss.

- We needed them to be loving, and they were not. That's a
  loss.

- We needed them to believe in us, and they did not. That's
  a loss.

- We needed them to be there for us, and they were not.
  That's a loss.

- We ended up believing (falsely) that the defect was in us.
  That's a loss.

Grieving can move us out of the posture of being stuck in life and
into the experience of true freedom in Christ.

We can grieve ourselves out of fear, which is the death of feeling safe.

We can grieve ourselves out of shame, which is the death of feeling worthy.

We can grieve ourselves out of depression, which is the death of feeling fully alive.[10]

We can grieve our losses, which is the death of being stuck.

And we're not grieving by ourselves. We are not alone—God is with us every step of the way.

What steps can we take to deal with these intangible losses that are so real to us? Identify the loss and give it a name. Call it what it was. Remember, other people don't have to recognize or validate the loss. It's still a loss for us. Understand that the reason we've experienced this loss is not because of a defect within us. What is wrong is what happened to us that was negative. If the trauma happened in childhood, we were not responsible.

The more we can learn about our pasts, our losses, and how others survive and grow through similar experiences, the easier it becomes to recognize, identify, validate, and accept our emotions. This might mean not accepting what others have said about their own grief or ours. The reality is that we were created by God as emotional beings. Emotions are a gift. Everyone occasionally experiences a mixture of emotions that are uncomfortable or disturbing. And that's okay.

Finally, we need to say goodbye to whatever or whomever we've lost. A good step in the grief process is writing a "Letting Go" letter. A letter such as this generates feelings, but releases them as well. It moves us along the recovery process and brings healing. Write the letter instead of inputting it electronically. This opens the door to drawing out more emotion. If our loss was a person, we can talk about one of the special times we experienced together, what we miss, what we wish, what we wish we could still talk about, and what has been most difficult for us during this time of grief. These subjects may bring up others. We can conclude our letter by stating that we're in the process of letting go and experiencing life again. Remember, keep this an honest expression. Then we need to read the letter out loud to ourselves or to a trusted friend.

Grieving Takes Time

Perhaps we've been in our grief process for a while. There are two questions that will need to be addressed at some time. Have we committed ourselves to a certain amount of time to grieve? Some do so unintentionally, and some do intentionally. Don't let any of these suggested time frames dictate recovery time. Don't set a time frame unless it's all the time you need. Keep it open-ended.

Have we given ourselves permission to stop grieving at a given point in time in the future? Consider this: People in grief need to give themselves permission to grieve and permission to stop grieving. Throughout grief, we say goodbye to the one or what we lost. Eventually we say hello to something new or different.

> Forgive. When we release the person, we too are released.

Some goodbyes carry a sense of sadness, a feeling of "I wish it wasn't so." The word "goodbye" was originally based on "God be with you" or "Go with God." It was a recognition that God was a significant part of the going. Perhaps we've forgotten that along with the journey, we gain strength when we remember that the Giver of life is here to protect and console, especially when the going is because of a death.[11]

Goodbyes can create an empty place within us. But with some goodbyes, we may feel a sense of relief or even joy because the parting should have occurred a long time ago.

If we express relief over the loss of a person, some people may not understand because they don't have the same relationship we experienced. The author of *Praying Our Goodbyes* wrote:

> We all need to learn to say goodbye, acknowledge the pain that is there for us so we can eventually move on to another hello. When we learn to say goodbye, we truly learn how to say to ourselves and to others: Go. God be with you. I entrust you to God. The God of strength, courage, comfort, hope, love is with you. The God who promises to wipe away all tears will hold you close and will fill your emptiness. Let go and be free to move on. Do not keep yourself from another step in your homeward journey. May the blessing of our God be with you.[12]

One of the most common barriers to completing grief over any loss is the "if only..." statement. "If only I..." or "If only it could have been different." Some say to get rid of "if only" statements, but it can be helpful to dream about the way we think it could have been because it helps us identify all the things we lost. No one else will do this for us, so we need to take this step and think about our past. We can do this a number of ways. We can write a story about the way we think it should have been or we can complete a series of "I wish..." statements:

- I wish my _____ had...
- I wish my _____ hadn't...
- I wish my _____ had said...
- I wish my _____ hadn't said...
- I wish my _____ would say to me today...
- I wish my _____ wouldn't say to me today...

For grief to be complete and for goodbyes to bring closure, there is one other step that has been mentioned on more than one occasion in this book. It's called forgiveness. Perhaps we have unfinished business that causes us to cling to hurts and offenses by the one who died. Some people carry vivid recollections of past events. They bear the offenses of the other person as a burden. We inflict inner torment on ourselves when we refuse to let go. The solution? Forgive. When we release the person, we too are released. If we don't forgive, we sentence ourselves to the prison of resentment. Lewis Smedes said it well:

> When you forgive someone for hurting you, you perform spiritual surgery inside your soul; you cut away the wrong that was done to you so that you can see your "enemy" through the magic eyes that can heal your soul. Detach that person from the hurt and let it go, the way children open their hands and let a trapped butterfly go free.
>
> Then invite that person back into your mind, fresh, as if a piece of history between you had been erased, its grip on your memory broken. Reverse the seemingly irreversible flow of pain within you.[13]

We are able to forgive because God has forgiven us. One of the best definitions of forgiveness is "wishing the other person well." It involves letting go. It's like holding a pen tightly in your hand and then opening your hand and watching the pen drop to the floor. Remember playing tug-of-war as a child? As long as the parties on each end of the rope were tugging, we had a "war." But when one side let go, the war was over. When we forgive, we are letting go of our end of the rope. No matter how hard the person may tug on the other end, if we have released the rope, the war is over.

Here are some statements people have made about releasing someone:

- I release you from determining how I respond to others in my life.

- I release you from the anger and resentment I've held toward you and others in my life because of you.

- I no longer hold you responsible for my happiness. I release you from my expectations of who you should have been, what you should have done, and...

- I release you from not being there for me emotionally and for your silence over the years. I don't know why you weren't there. I don't need to know.

- I was mad at you for dying when I was a child and not giving me a chance to get to know you. I missed out on so much. I blamed you. I'm sorry. I hope you're in heaven.

- I forgive you.

Too many individuals have stopped listening to their feelings. They've ignored them or tried to make them disappear. It doesn't work.

The Value of Loss

We've all heard the question, "Who in your life has impacted you or brought about change in your life?" I suggest going beyond that and asking, "How did that come about?" For me, one of the greatest

life changes has been through the printed word—mainly books. Ken
Gire's books *Windows of the Soul* and *The Divine Embrace* are two I've
gotten a lot from. Since reading *Reflections on the Movies*, also by Ken
Gire. I watch movies differently now. In that book Ken suggested that
whenever we watch a movie, we should look for the theme of redemption. In most films, without stretching the issue, we can see a plan of
redemption unfold.

I've taken that concept and applied it to the purpose of loss. Loss is
a painful experience, and yet there can be value, meaning, and growth
through the experience. Probably not at first, but eventually there is a
discovery of redemption. So with each loss, we need to look beyond
the pain to discover what at first may seem hidden. Many people are
destroyed by loss because they choose to wallow in the guilt and anger
of what could have been or what they failed at doing. They become bitter in spirit or fall into despair.

In loss, we often can't change the situation, but we can allow the situation to change us. We exacerbate our suffering needlessly when we
allow one loss to domino into another. That causes gradual destruction
of the soul, which is the tragedy called the "second death."

Worse still is the *death of the spirit*—the death that comes through
guilt, regret, bitterness, hatred, immorality, and despair. The first kind
of death happens *to* us; the second kind of death happens *in* us. The
deaths after the first loss are ones we bring on ourselves if we refuse to
be transformed by the first death—to grieve the loss and then move
forward.

Regret can also lead to transformation if we view loss as an opportunity to take inventory of our lives. Loss forces us to see ourselves for
who we are.

Loss can also be transformative if we set a new course for our lives.

Finally, loss can be transformative if it causes us to seek the forgiveness of God. Sometimes our stalled forward motion reminds us of how
far short we fell prior to the loss and how insincerely we responded to it.
The snapshot exposes our inner selves. We are forced to face any ugliness, selfishness, and meanness in ourselves. Then what? In the case of
loss, there is no second chance. We're left only with a bitter memory of

our failures or even the good intentions we had but failed to live up to. But God promises to forgive those of us who confess our failures, to absolve those of us who confess our guilt, and to make right what we are sorry for doing wrong.[14]

Maybe it will lessen our discomfort some if we replace the word "losses" with the word "endings." We all have a life history of those. Some people deny endings; some delay them; some try to minimize their significance. Some tend to believe that things simply will happen as they happen, no matter what. Often, when people talk about endings or losses, even if they're moving on, they're past-focused. That is, though they have a new future, their focus is still on the ending. "I lost… six months ago…a year ago… three years ago." When we do this, what might happen in terms of our hope, our optimism, even our joy? What if instead of (or in addition to) saying, *"That* ended…" we said, *"This* started"? That's not ignoring or denying the ending, but it's conveying that we won't let the loss consume our lives. We won't permit it to keep us from heading forward. We can fixate on endings…or we can focus on beginnings. Accepting the ending of a phase *is* a beginning.[15]

The next suggestion may sound different, but it has changed lives for the better. When we recognize and identify our losses, we also need to identify what is not lost. There are certain parts of our lives that have not been lost that can help put a different perspective on the past and how it relates to our present. This isn't a form of denial or a negation of what we experienced. Every one of us has strengths and inner resources that can be used for the process of change. Even if our losses have limited us in some areas, there are still possibilities and existing strengths we can use. After we list what we haven't lost, we can see our strengths and what we have in spite of the loss. When we notice our blessings, we can thank God for them and ask Him to use these to help us imagine the possibilities.

> Because God is the ultimate sufferer; he is the ultimate One to whom we can turn when we suffer. Because he has borne the grief of millions, he can bear our grief as well. He can handle our anger, our rage, our shame, our guilt. He

will hear our cries, he will hold us in our weeping, he will
listen to our questions. And ultimately he will wipe away
our tears...

God doesn't only absorb the pain of grief and loss; he makes
a way through it. Because suffering is within the realm of
God's comprehension and knowledge, it becomes a point
of contact between us and God.[16]

We may wish our lives will turn out to match our dreams and that
there will be complete healing and positive changes. We can't change
others, though, and we can't alter some of the factors existing in our
environment. We need to carve out a new normal. We need to focus
on making internal changes. We need to look for what is possible and
realistic rather than unobtainable ideals.[17]

Chapter 8

Trauma and Our Past

Trauma. It began with Adam and Eve. Their act of disobedience led to their banishment and the ensuing consequences. The losses they experienced were life-changing and overwhelming (Genesis 3). And, as often happens, when trauma touches one family, there is a ripple effect on other members. Adam and Eve's direct descendant Cain murdered his brother Abel. Any event that shatters our world so that it's no longer a place of refuge is trauma. It's more than a state of crisis. It is a normal reaction to abnormal events that overwhelm a person's ability to adapt to life. We feel powerless.

Why do we need to know about trauma? What if we believe we've never experienced something drastic like trauma, yet we know something isn't quite right? Perhaps that's true. But perhaps we aren't recognizing trauma. It occurs anytime we believe our world is no longer safe. What we used to see as predictable no longer is.

Most people overestimate the likelihood that their lives are going to be relatively free from major crises or traumas. They underestimate the possibility of negative events happening to them. People never dream that the things that happen to them were ever going to happen. Perhaps that's why they're so devastated when the bad things occur.

Trauma and Beliefs

So, what beliefs do we hold about life? What will happen to those beliefs if we experience trauma? It's important to ask ourselves these questions before the next trauma comes. If we live with a feeling of invulnerability, the "it can't happen to me" mentality, trauma will not only wound us by destroying this belief, but it will also fill our lives with fear. Invulnerability is an illusion.

Trauma comes in different shapes and sizes, encompassing a vast array of human experiences. It's "one of the most common causes of illness. It has incredible power to open the doors of our bodies to sickness. When you experience something traumatic, it's kind of like an emotional earthquake in your body. It causes everything to 'shift,' and not in a good way."[1]

The word "trauma" comes from a Greek word that means "wound." It's a condition characterized by the phrase "I just can't seem to get over it." If you've ever been to a rodeo, you've probably seen riders pursuing steers. In the competition, a rider guides the horse next to the galloping steer's horns, leaps off the horse, grabs the horns, and with the right amount of pressure at the right time, throws the steer to the ground. When we experience trauma, it's like we're thrown about like that steer. Our world turns wild, out of control, crazy. Trauma untreated or ignored may last for years or even a lifetime.

The wounds of trauma can create a condition called post-traumatic stress disorder (PTSD). The effects of trauma aren't just emotional responses to troubling events. They can cause a persistent deregulation of body and brain chemistry. And brain chemistry can be altered for decades. Why do trauma's effects linger? Because they are the result of a reorganization of the central nervous system after we've experienced an actual threat of annihilation.[2]

Trauma creates chaos in our brains and causes an emotional as well as a cognitive concussion. Entering the world of trauma is like looking into a fractured looking glass. The familiar appears disjointed and disturbing; a strange new world unfolds. "In normal time, we move from one moment to the next, sunrise to sunset, birth to death. After trauma, we may move in circles, find ourselves being sucked backward into an eddy, or bouncing about like a rubber ball from now to then, and back again."[3]

The "post" in post-traumatic stress disorder means just that. The hyper alertness, the fear, the anxiety, the sweating, the psychic numbing, the emotional distancing in the present moment are all the direct result of something that happened in the past. In simple terms, what we experienced was too great, too alien, and too powerful to be comprehended and understood by us at the moment. So the trauma sits there tucked away, but it's still active until it is driven into the present moment to be dealt with. At times, trauma can be a massive eruption. At other times, it moves in silently over an extended period of time, until its fury has overtaken the present moment.

People who have experienced trauma have difficulty understanding what is going on when they're revisited by the trauma from their past. To most of them, this is the closest thing to being insane. Jim described his experience to me:

> I have good days, but then when it hits, I have difficulty accepting this is happening to me. It's someone else, or I'm someone else. I see, I hear, I smell, I taste, I feel the past. I believe I'm nuts. I've got to be crazy. When you see what others do not see, when you smell what others do not smell, when you hear what others do not hear, the conclusion you reach is that you must be mentally ill.

But trauma survivors aren't. We experience a normal response to something that was beyond our ability to handle. When traumatized people talk about their past, they often recount events in a detached, monotone voice, seemingly without emotion. They end their stories by saying, "But that is all in the past. I don't let it bother me now." They deny that the trauma has any present impact. That's how they keep the last trauma at bay. They live their lives in what can be described as "quiet desperation" and in significant distance from others. They may "be with people," but in reality they're really not completely present.

People with unresolved trauma numb their emotions and avoid at all costs anything that might trigger the memories of the traumatic event. Shutting down—and staying that way—requires most of their energy. It's exhausting. They believe the lid must be kept on the past no matter what. So they continue to live in the past, whether the event occurred at age three or thirty. The emotions that do damage might be rage and anger. These are often misdirected "out there" at whatever and whoever happens by—the elderly person driving in the slow-moving vehicle, the teenager with the purple hair and multiple piercings, or the government. In these ways, trauma has its own opportunities for expression. It is seldom direct, but it has a daily effect on the quality of life of the people involved. It affects mood, feelings, actions, and, above all, relationships. People may touch the surface of the pain, but the actual trauma isn't dealt with constructively. Its place is just beyond the range of daily activity.

The old moment is relived physically, emotionally, and spiritually, not just remembered. "PTSD is having memories you don't want to have. It's being led by the worst part of your memory."[4] This is emotional remembering, not historical remembering. What was buried in the mind doesn't tell time. When it projects this "alien" material from the past onto the present moment, the time is both *then* and *now.* It's confusing to everyone, especially the traumatized one.[5]

If we were traumatized, when something reminds us of the past, our right brain reacts as if the traumatic event were happening in the present, in the now. Because our left brain, the analytical side, isn't working very well, we may not be aware that we're reexperiencing and reacting to the past. We might just know we're furious, terrified, enraged, ashamed, or frozen. After the emotional storm passes, we may look for something or somebody to blame for the outburst.[6]

One of the characteristics of trauma is it creates unchangeable feelings, thoughts, and behaviors. We feel like they're cast in stone. Trauma changes us. As we've discussed, the changes take place in our brains. What is unique about the control trauma has on our past is that traumatization is really about being trapped in the uncompleted act of escape. Any event or situation that generates emotion is a stressor that changes the chemicals in our brain. But if it's a traumatized event, a permanent imbalance is created in our brains. It's as though it was tattooed on our brain. Trauma is like a blister on the right side of the brain. *With trauma, the past is always present.*[7] When I have shared this with some individuals, they rose from their chair and yelled, "That's it! That's exactly what it's like."

Trauma attacks who we are. It attacks our identity and disassembles who we are so we have to build new identities even though some of the old remains. "Chief among the crimes that trauma commits against the mind is the distortions of memory it introduces. In the face of terror, the mind skips straight over some things and perversely over-records others.[8]

How do we know if we've been traumatized or have PTSD? Think of this as a group of three clusters.

The first PTSD cluster is symptoms. We respond to symptoms when aspects of the traumatic event are relived in some way. A common one is a flashback. We relive the trauma as though it is happening here and now. The best description I know of a flashback came from a nurse: "I want to tell you what a flashback is like. It is as if time is folded or warped, so that the past and present merge, as if I were physically trans-ported into the past."[9]

There are other symptoms, which include nightmares, visual images, emotions of intense fear, or anxieties or intrusive thoughts.

The second cluster is avoidance. We try to stay away from anything that could trigger a reexperiencing of symptoms. Many people spend their time and energy avoiding this fight, but usually they're unsuccessful.

The third cluster is hyperarousal. We're constantly on alert. Our nervous system is always excited. Intensive anxiety, anger, or instability is part of our life.[10]

Trauma comes from so many sources. Childhood itself can be a source resulting from lack of attachment and nurturing. All through life there are potential causes, including accidents, bullying, name-calling, learning or physically disabled, estrangement, any kind of loss, cultural traditions, and media reporting.

The worst experience for a young child is neglect because it affects every part of the developing neurological system. When a child is born, neurons in the brain are ready to be stimulated and put into use. This promotes growth in the brain. But if there is chronic neglect, this process is interrupted and distorted.

A child can be impacted by trauma even before they're born. A mother's emotional state can affect her unborn child. If a mother experiences chronic stress during her pregnancy, stress hormones are passed on through the bloodstream to the fetus. An increase in cortisol in the mother is shared with the unborn child. Not only that, but stress can reduce the blood and oxygen supply to the fetus.

Once a child is born, there were two things needed more than anything else for emotional development: touch and eye contact. If this is lacking, the brain is impacted and emotional development is lacking.[11] As a child, when we responded or reacted in a certain way because of past damage, others may have berated us for the way we behaved or spoke. And yet, based on what we experienced, our response was normal. Few people really understand the impact of constant verbal and emotional abuse children may suffer. When we live in an abusive environment, we often end up judging ourselves as defective in some way.

What happens when we hear constant criticism and abuse? Naturally, we repeat it to ourselves and believe it's true. This creates pathways in our brains that program the negativity in as part of our core beliefs. If people, especially adults, attacked you, they must be right. We pick up the tools and continue the personal attacks on ourselves. One of the worst experiences of life is emotional abandonment. It's one thing to have one or two people who emotionally abuse us, but when we don't have a single caretaker to turn to when we need someone it's devastating. The younger we were and the longer the abuse went on the greater the impact. As one therapist said: "Growing up emotionally neglected is like nearly dying of thirst outside the fenced off fountain of a person's warmth and interest. Emotional neglect makes children feel worthless, unlovable, excruciatingly empathic. They starve for human warmth and comfort."[12]

> Any new experience similar to the original event results in that same traumatic response.

Trauma literally rewires the brain. It could be a death, an accident, physical or sexual abuse, neglect, or something else. If trauma occurs during early childhood, there are several results, including overdeveloping some of the neural networks related to survival and retarding some aspects of growth, such as emotional development.

One of the ways the brain responds to trauma is through imprinting.

The more extensive the trauma and the more frequently it occurs, the more of an imprint or indelible impression is left within the brain. Someone described trauma as "tattooing the experience on the brain." This imprint becomes the processing template for new information. Its effects are like this:

> Imagine the brain as a large valley with a river running through it. Several streams converge into the river. Those are like the pathways in the brain. When a rainstorm—normal negative event—rips through the valley, the excess water flows in a predictable direction. It finds its way to creeks, then streams, and then converges into the river. But sometimes there is a massive storm that has so much rain, the runoff goes beyond existing channels and creates a new path outside the streams. It may even alter the course of the river in some way. Once the river has been changed, it tends to stay that way, until a more intense storm establishes a new channel.
>
> In a similar way, everyday normal experiences come into the brain and find their way to existing networks of processing templates. All that changes if an overwhelming storm occurs. After that, alterations occur in thinking.
>
> Childhood trauma is the equivalent of the 100-year flood.[13]

With trauma, new pathways, new imprints, are formed. Our thinking process is changed forever unless constructive steps are taken, usually through therapy, to reverse the damage. When children are traumatized, their brains form around the experiences. The experience is coded into neural templates. Any new experience similar to the original event results in that same traumatic response.

How does this relate to our core beliefs and subsequent thoughts? Imagine that you're a small child. At an early age you hear negative messages: "You're no good," "You're so awkward," "You can't be trusted," "You'll never amount to much." These negative messages continue over and over, week after week, month after month, year after year. Even if you hear them only occasionally, there's a negative impact. Constant rejection eventually creates a powerful neural pathway. It's as though a groove is gradually worn into the memory banks of your brain, and you begin to believe this is reality. It becomes a core belief that shapes your thoughts and self-talk about who you are.

Childhood loss and trauma shape our lives. The types of losses and trauma have much to say about how our lives are shaped. A few years ago I was watching a television show that was interrupted by a live news report about an enraged man on a Los Angeles freeway. As the news cameras rolled, thousands of people watched in horror as this man waved a shotgun in the air and threatened to kill himself. Like everyone watching that day, I prayed and hoped for a peaceful solution. But I also said out loud, "Stop the cameras! This man is going to shoot himself, and thousands of people, including hundreds of children, will have a scene of graphic violence etched in their minds for years to come. Please have some sense and turn off the cameras." Unfortunately, they didn't. We can be traumatized by personally experiencing it or getting it as a secondary trauma. The latter is observing it, like watching the image of the planes striking the World Trade Center towers and the Pentagon or the man who took his life on TV. We may not even realize the extent of the trauma being inflicted.

One of the worst types of trauma is called "complex" because it is just that. Complex usually refers to traumatic experiences that are interpersonal. They are caused by other individuals. They are premeditated by adults. And they usually occur on a continual basis. To add to the intensity, often the perpetrator is a family member or family friend. On top of the trauma, there is now betrayal and violation. The victims, usually children, feel trapped. Where do they go for help? Traumas such as these usually impact us more than natural disasters or accidents. The more impersonal the trauma, the less effect it has on us.

The abuse that occurs by a parent or family friend is the most common. Often those doing the traumatizing were traumatized when they were young. Unfortunately, this type of trauma occurs at vulnerable times developmentally, such as early childhood or adolescence.[14] Consistent emotional abuse can be just as devastating as physical and/or sexual abuse.

To live with chronic abuse is to live in silence, to be shut up. The spirit of those so abused have been crushed. The victims become immobilized by intense fear and silenced by the deafness of others. What is the point of speaking when no one will listen? The victims are shut up by the threat of abandonment, which will surely come if they get in the way or say too much.[15]

If you're a childhood trauma victim, you will find your past continually intruding on your present. You will find the trauma repeatedly interrupting life. It will feel as if both present and future have been swallowed up by the past, and they break in without warning, in flashbacks when you're awake and in nightmares when you're asleep. Triggers in the form of smells or sounds can evoke memories that return with all the emotional force and physiological responses that accompanied the original event.[16]

The wisdom of Scripture is so evident in all of these types of issues. "Fathers, do not embitter your children, or they will become discouraged" (Colossians 3:21). The Amplified Version of the Bible puts it this way: "Fathers, do not provoke or irritate or exasperate your children [with demands that are trivial or unreasonable or humiliating or abusive; nor by favoritism or indifference; treat them tenderly with lovingkindness], so they will not lose heart and become discouraged or unmotivated [with their spirits broken]."

Violating this scripture can contribute to one of the worst traumas for any child: emotional neglect. This is a major factor in the life and experiences of most traumatized children. Too often parents ignore or reject a child's call for attention or help or even wanting a close relationship. This form of abandonment feeds a child's fear and diminishes his or her feeling of hope. These children often blame themselves and take on the responsibility for something that wasn't their fault.

Our Damaged Pasts

If emotional or physical abuse is in our past, there is a word that is important for us to know: "dissociation." Many people with damaged pasts have experienced this in one way or another. It's one of the most common responses to a traumatic situation. Basically, it's a feeling of being "not all here." Our bodies may be present, but the rest of us isn't. Physically present; psychologically not present.

Perhaps you were out driving and you can't remember the last ten blocks. Or you might start doing something routine you've done hundreds of times, but this time you forget the next step. Your thinking process at this time feels different. It's sluggish and definitely not sharp. Dissociation is a common occurrence for all of us in our everyday lives. Have you ever sat through a boring lecture and your mind wandered to other places and thoughts? All of a sudden your mind returns to the lecture and you realize you've missed the last fifteen minutes? That's dissociation. Or have you ever taken a trip, driving for several hours, and upon arrival at your destination you have no memory of several segments of the trip? That's dissociation. Our interstate highway system was deliberately constructed with occasional curves to keep us from falling into a trance state described as "highway hypnosis."

Dissociating becomes a problem when it interferes with the present. During trauma, dissociation may have been the wisest and safest thing for us to do at the time. The problem is that dissociation tends to work so well that we keep it up and use it as a constant coping mechanism. Dissociation is also referred to as splitting. This involves leaving—physically or emotionally. We might not even be aware we're doing it.

Dissociation also shows up in the sense of feeling disconnected from what is happening—emotionally numb, maybe like "it's not really happening to me," or like we're watching a movie. We're "elsewhere." We do this to feel safe. Sometimes it may be a blessed release from the pain or terror.

When we've experienced trauma, part of us may still be frozen in that past trauma, which means part of our system's capacity is unavailable. Part of us is then and there, not here and now.[17] "Traumatized people chronically feel unsafe inside their body. The past is alive in the form of gnawing interior discomfort."[18]

People learn to dissociate, especially with childhood trauma. It was a survival technique during or after trauma, and it served to protect us. It was an attempt to feel safe, but usually people feel less safe when it's occurring. Many who experienced early childhood abuse of some form learned to dissociate.[19] It could have been wise and safe then, but now it probably isn't. It keeps us from working on and resolving the trauma and its symptoms.

We all differ in our coping skills. Sometimes there is no easy explanation for many of the differences. Some individuals seem to naturally be more dissociative than others. We probably all have this ability to some degree, although trauma and abuse intensifies the effects and use. What can we do? It's time to take charge. How? By controlling or planning dissociation. Yes, it sounds strange, yet this is a way of gaining control or power over what was an automatic survival technique. One technique is to identify one or two imaginary safe places that are accessible to us. When we're frightened or anxious, we purposely go to one of our imagined places. After being there for a while, we'll write out why we felt safe there and what feelings we were experiencing. We may resist this exercise since we'll probably feel uncomfortable. That's all right. Keep in the present. (The Ball of Grief in chapter 4 may help identify specific emotions.)

It's normal not to want to feel pain associated with traumatic experiences. But keeping feelings and memories beyond our conscious awareness can create difficulties in other parts of life. Dissociation interferes with our relationship with ourselves. It gets in the way of enjoying time spent alone, comforting ourselves, feeling good about ourselves, and tolerating our strong feelings. Shutting down negative feelings usually constricts positive feelings as well. Opening ourselves to facing and feeling pain gradually can open us to feeling more joy. Feeling anger can help generate energy for healing projects and changing unacceptable conditions.[20]

Many of the most distressing elements of the traumatic wound are based on the need to keep memories of the trauma out of consciousness. "Refriending" the memory by claiming its reality is a significant step in alleviating symptoms and making meaning of the traumatic event. The desire to keep the trauma contained and at bay by building right up to its edges with the hope of containment or running so fast that feelings can't catch up is powerful and restrictive. It may work for a while, but memory that is not paid honor or heeded will find other ways to make its presence known. Have you ever had a song stuck in your mind which plays over and over again? Almost all of us have experienced this at one time or another.

One of the characteristics of trauma is disturbing intrusive thoughts or images which intrude into your mind seemingly out of nowhere. They are considered intrusive when they are disturbing and repetitive. Most people try to keep the thoughts from occurring, which doesn't really work. What does seem to work for many is to 1) invite the thoughts in and state "You are disturbing, but I can handle you"; 2) have another scenario available to think about to replace the thought; or 3) write out the thoughts in detail, read it out loud again and again, and each time, change some part of them.[21]

Most who have been abused or emotionally neglected or abandoned as children have never grieved the loss of their childhoods. It could be that no one has ever suggested they need to grieve these losses.

There are three factors that contribute to a person being stuck in their past by trauma:

- The trauma is repetitive.
- The trauma is ongoing.
- There is no help.

Do any of these fit your childhood experiences? If so, the past could still be present.

The author of *Transforming Trauma* suggested a number of helpful questions to assist us in identifying this issue in our lives. They may help us find out more about our patterns of dissociation. These questions are meant to be an awareness builder, not a test…and certainly not a reason to self-criticize.

- What parts of your body are most difficult to feel when you try to bring your attention to them?
- Do you sometimes totally lose track of what another person is saying or find it hard to comprehend what should be simple? Do you have periods when you can't concentrate or think at all?

- Do you sometimes have a sense of unreality, where things don't seem quite real?

- Do you bump into things a lot?

- Do you ever get that thick, paralyzed feeling?

- Do you sometimes feel confused about time and place, as if waking up out of a fog?

- Has anyone ever said you look spaced out, as if you were somewhere else?[22]

The loss of future is certainly connected with loss of hope, but perhaps the two need to be kept separate for a better assessment of our spiritual condition. Loss of future is, perhaps, more subtle than loss of hope. It is reflected in those bits of convention that create an uncomfortable feeling in the listener: "Just pack me off to the nursing home when the kids are finished with me"; "There is no sense in retiring. There would certainly be nothing to do"; "No sense in having kids in this world"; "It's crazy to make plans. Somebody always messes them up"; "They never let you do what you want to do"; "Life is just the same thing each day."

These are the words of people who have lost their future, so the future has no meaning to them. It is nothing but the repetition of today or worse. At some level, however, there must be the fear that to give tomorrow any power is to also give it the power to re-create the past. The future, therefore, must be envisioned as powerless or, at least, to make it have less power than yesterday. The loss of future is the wish to make the world stand still so it creates no further harm. It is the wish to be left alone.[23]

One of the forms of denial that often occurs with an intense traumatic experience is "it never happened." We live with the hope that we just dreamed, or imagined, or didn't experience what happened. It's hoping and praying and saying, "It didn't happen!" The longer this goes on, the more this seems true since our memories diminish with time. But there's always that nagging feeling that the trauma could have happened. Some people will admit that it happened, but insist it didn't affect them long term. The reality is these "would be" experiences and events would impact anyone. But we find reasons not to consider the impact of the trauma or its lasting consequences.

Yet another response is to downplay the impact on ourselves. "You know, it's too bad that happened, but it's not that big a deal." But it was. "It wasn't that significant." We admit to what happened, but quickly add, "It could have been worse." We give one example after another as to how it could have been worse. It's called minimizing. "The trauma happened and used to affect me, but I'm over it and moving on with my life." If that were only true. This is one of the most common responses. This belief limits our growth and our ability to move ahead. We want to be "over it," but it's hidden behind a wall. Healing won't occur without facing and identifying what occurred and working through the pain.

Many counselees have told me the reason for their avoidance is the belief that if they talk about it, they will get upset. What happens when we experience an overwhelming loss or trauma? There are at least two results stemming from this experience. One can be the disruption and shattering of our world. The other can be a shift from a meaningless life and existence to the creation of a meaningful life. During the journey and traumatization, there will be times of disillusionment.

There are some trauma survivors who cope; there are some trauma survivors who cope well. The ones who grow during this time do so not because of their losses and trauma, but, strangely enough, by the creation of value and meaning because of their losses—especially the loss of some of their beliefs and illusions. It's reminiscent of the wisdom in James 1:2-3: "Consider it pure joy, my brothers and sisters, whenever you face trials of many kinds, because you know that the testing of your faith produces perseverance."[24]

Remember, trauma is not a life sentence. There is hope.

Chapter 9

Putting Past Trauma Behind Us

Where do we go from here to move forward to live in the present and future as God intends for us to live? As we explore suggestions and ideas for dealing with our trauma, remember that what helps one person might not help another. As we read, let's ask God to direct us and give us wisdom and discernment in what He wants us to know and do.

Here are three specific goals to work toward to alleviate trauma and its effects. The first is to take our thoughts about our traumatic experience and see them in a new way. Reframe them so they are more accurate and healthy. This means we must uncover the underlying fear or hurt.

The second goal is to lessen our emotional responses to and involvement in the trauma.

Finally, we need to carefully and cautiously expose ourselves to the trauma and discover new, healthy ways of handling our emotions and eliminate unhealthy behaviors.

Here are some key thoughts to remember about trauma:

- Being traumatized is not incurable. Recovery is possible, but it is a slow process.

- We will probably need to work with a professional— someone who is equipped to assist those experiencing and dealing with trauma.

- We can promote healing through understanding. The more we learn about trauma for ourselves and others, the more we'll feel in control of our lives.

There is another side to trauma to watch for. Current research on those traumatized indicates the majority of victims say they eventually *benefited from the trauma* in some way. And these people experienced as much pain as those who didn't fully recover. How did they benefit? There was a change of values, a greater appreciation for life, a deepening of spiritual beliefs, a feeling of greater strength and appreciation, and a building of relationships. The most important elements in recovering are to remain connected to people, to develop a strong personal relationship with Jesus, and to apply the Scriptures to our lives.[1]

For healing to occur, we need to stop seeing ourselves as people who are diseased or deficient. We need to not refer to ourselves as traumatized people. We are not abnormal because of our trauma symptoms. The event(s) that we experienced were abnormal. The event was so out of the ordinary that it overwhelmed us, as it would anyone.

Letting Jesus Help

Perhaps you've heard the saying, "I took it to the cross" or "Take it to the foot of the cross." This is an expression of giving what we're struggling with to our Lord Jesus Christ. This is not a ritual but a way to experience sharing with God and beginning to heal our past and our pain. We can do this by ourselves or with a person we trust.

There are different ways this can be done. We can make a cross out of wood or cardboard or draw a cross on a large box. Grab a pen and some paper. And then:

> Take time alone and ask God to show you the painful things that are buried deep in your heart. Which ones are most painful? Which memories do you not like to think about? Write these down. Be as specific as possible. You should write down the worst things that you remember, such as:
>
> - Bad things that have been done to you
> - Bad things you have seen done to others or bad dreams you have had
> - Bad things that you may have done to others

Read the following passage out loud:

> But he endured the suffering that should have been ours,
>   the pain that we should have borne.
> All the while we thought that his suffering
>   was punishment sent by God.
> But because of our sins he was wounded,
>   beaten because of the evil we did.
> We are healed by the punishment he suffered,
>   made whole by the blows he received.
> All of us were like sheep that were lost,
>   each of us going his own way.
> But the Lord made the punishment fall on him,
>   the punishment all of us deserved (Isaiah 53:4-7 GNT).

Then take them outside and read Isaiah 61:1-3 aloud:

> The Sovereign LORD has filled me with his Spirit.
> He has chosen me and sent me
> To bring good news to the poor;
> To heal the broken-hearted,
> To announce release to captives
> And freedom to those in prison.
> He has sent me to proclaim
> That the time has come
> When the LORD will save his people
> And defeat their enemies.
> He has sent me to comfort all who mourn,
> To give to those who mourn in Zion
> Joy and gladness instead of grief,
> A song of praise instead of sorrow.
> They will be like trees
> That the LORD himself has planted.
> They will all do what is right,
> And God will be praised for what he has done (GNT).

Burn the papers to show that the suffering you have experienced has become like ashes. This can be a time of experiencing God's healing.[2]

Here are some useful messages for nurturing the growth of our self-compassion and self-esteem. I recommend that we imagine speaking them to our "inner child," especially if we're suffering flashbacks. We needed to hear these truths as children. Unfortunately, many of us never did. Take this list, stand in front of a mirror, and read them out loud with emphasis. We need to do this again and again.

- I am so glad you were born.
- You are a good person.
- I love who you are, and I'm doing my best to always be on your side.
- You can come to me whenever you're feeling hurt or bad.
- You do not have to be perfect to get my love and protection.
- All of your feelings are okay with me.
- I am always glad to see you.
- It is okay for you to be angry. I won't let you hurt yourself or others when you are.
- You can make mistakes—they are your teachers.
- You can know what you need and ask for help.
- You can have your own preferences and tastes.
- You are a delight to my eyes.
- You can choose your own values.
- You can pick your own friends, and you don't have to like everyone.
- You can sometimes feel confused, ambivalent, and not know all the answers.
- I am very proud of you.[3]

Why Should We Tell Our Stories?

For many traumatized people, it's tempting not to confront our pain and tell our story. Like sandbags in a flood, they keep the murky waters of pain away from our hearts. So why would anyone want to remove the sandbags and let the waters flow in? Isn't that just too risky and maybe even foolish? Why should we open up?

First, we tell our stories because the trauma won't go away by itself. The waves of trauma may recede like floodwaters, but like floodwaters, they also leave a path of hurt and destruction.

There's a second important reason to tell our story: Sharing the story starts the healing process. On one level, sharing our story will "lift the veil of denial, mystery, and silence" that so often shrouds trauma.

> Sharing helps us as well as those around us.

The events of the trauma—the sights, sounds, feelings, smells—may seem like a random jumble of an automobile junkyard. By sharing the story, we start to organize the jumble of sensations, making sense out of the senselessness.

I like the way this author described the purpose of sharing:

> Telling the story is a form of lament, or ordering our grief. It helps us process the events and move beyond denial. When we tell the story, whether speaking out loud or writing on paper, we confront ourselves with the reality of the loss. We may say to others, "I can't believe this is happening, but here's what happened." Doing so helps us come to grips with the fact that the loss occurred. Telling the story prevents us from escaping into a fantasy world where nothing happened and everything is fine.
>
> Furthermore, telling the story helps others understand what we have experienced and how we are feeling. It gives them the opportunity to listen to us and share our grief.[4]

Sharing helps us as well as those around us.

Remembering and telling. At their own pace and in their own way, people need to be able to tell and retell their story as often as needed. Research shows that the act of telling one's story can help rewire the neural pathways of the brain affected by trauma. During trauma, ordinary connections between the right and left brain may diminish to help the person survive emotionally. The two sides become disconnected and function independently of one another. There is a purpose in this: We can function via the left brain with the facts of what is happening, and not be overcome by the feelings of fear or terror that would normally be associated with what happened.

We can't leave the brain in this state of distortion. If this gap is not reestablished eventually, it will leave us feeling alienated from our feelings and the feelings of others and of God. What can help? Telling our story, rebuilding a connection that is normal. The worst advice for us to hear is "just get better" or "forget it." This leads to frustration and despair. For us to tell our story, we need a safe relationship with someone who listens not just to our words but to us. This person needs to reflect the wisdom in Proverbs 18:13: "To answer before listening—that is folly and shame." If the person chosen criticizes, judges, or interrupts, we need to find someone else.

Consider these thoughts about our stories:

> Remembering, therefore, is not simply a function of the mind. It is an embedded expression of our lives as we recall the concrete, earthbound actions of God and people. It is an invitation to grace and adventure that involves all God's people. It is not just the past in our heads. It is the present in our doing.
>
> That is why I believe that faithfully telling and listening to our stories is one of the single most important things we can do as followers of Jesus. Storytelling inevitably engages our memories—both the speakers' and the hearers'—and so opens the door to a different future. The Bible is so powerful in part because it contains the *story* of creation, rebellion, redemption, and recreation, all of which are told in the rich, messy, beautiful, tragic, hopeful tapestry of the lives of God's ancient people.[5]

There are at least three levels to sharing our stories of past trauma. *First,* there is the heart level. We simply acknowledge to ourselves that we're carrying pain from past events. We realize that although we have said our prayers, read books, listened to sermons, attended Bible studies, and given it time, the pain hasn't healed. We've developed sophisticated mechanisms to hold the pain at bay, but the pain keeps oozing around our defensive walls.

Second, once we stop running into reasons not to share and, instead, attend to our hearts, we can move to the next level of getting our stories out: We become totally honest with God. The Bible tells us to "walk in the light" (1 John 1:7), part of which implies that we are totally transparent with God about our sin, our brokenness, our rage, our sadness, and our hurt.

Jesus is not the kind of High Priest who will say, "Get over it! Haven't you dealt with that trauma by now? What's taking you so long? And by the way, it didn't really hurt that bad, did it?" No, when Jesus looked at the crowds of hurting people, "He felt compassion for them, because they were distressed and dispirited like sheep without a shepherd" (Matthew 9:36 NASB).

Third, as we begin to tell our stories to our own hearts and in the presence of God, we can move to the last level of getting our stories out: We find safe people who will listen to our stories. At first we may find a friend, a small group, a therapy group, or a Christian counselor who will listen.

Here are some practical steps to remember as we move forward in telling our stories:

- *Go slow.* Don't feel pressured to get it out all in one session or one conversation. The healing path usually requires a long, slow journey with many steps.

- *Find someone you can trust.* Try out a little piece of your story and see how your listener responds. If he or she shuts you down, don't be discouraged. Sadly, some people cannot handle the pain or the jagged edges of trauma.

- *Don't worry about the details of your story.* Just start anywhere and don't worry about making sense. Often as you start talking and sharing your story, the details will start to fall into place.

- *Find a method of storytelling that fits you.* Poetry, drawing, painting, sculpture, writing, music, journaling, watching and discussing a film—there are many ways to get the story out.

- *Connect with a small group.* Hearing other stories of trauma and recovery will help you feel normal and help you create your own "new normal."

- *Be patient.* Telling your story does not bring instant healing. Sometimes it may start to bring more pain to the surface as you unfreeze the memories, bringing them out of the deep freeze of denial. This is normal. But remember you are on a new healing path. God will continue to guide the process.[6]

There is another process which is necessary in moving forward. Pete Walker called it *verbal ventilation.* I'm sure you've seen a ventilator at some time in your life. It's vital for the passage and movement of air.

> Verbal ventilation is speaking or writing in a manner that airs out and releases painful feelings. When we let our words spring from what we feel, language is imbued with emotion, and pain can be released through what we say, think or write. As our grieving proficiency increases, we can verbally ventilate about our losses.[7]

This approach is one that can impact and remediate brain changes caused by chronic PTSD. When we experience an emotional flashback, it over-activates the right brain, which is emotionally oriented, and under-activates the thinking-oriented left brain. Because of this, childhood pain reemerges because it's emotionally remembered by the memory-oriented right brain.

While this is occurring, we lose access to the thinking part of our brains—the left side. This is a temporary loss, but it makes it difficult for us to realize we're flashing back and not actually living the past again. We still feel helpless and hopeless. This is where verbal ventilation comes in. Its purpose is to bring left-brain thinking into the right-brain arena. This helps us develop the ability to put words to feelings and eventually communicate what we're feeling. When this is done often enough, new neural pathways develop that let the left and right sides of the brain work together, allowing us to think and feel at the same time. Research shows that our brains can generate new pathways between the two sides.[8]

What else can verbal ventilation accomplish for us in our journeys forward? We know we have two sides to our brain. Sometimes the right side is overly activated, and sometimes the left side is overly activated. The sides are meant to work together and balance each other. But sometimes one is reacting so much that the other side can't bring balance. Often when we've been abused or traumatized as children, our right side exerts its dominance through our emotions and feelings. What helps to bring balance? Verbal ventilation brings words to the feelings, and helps us interpret and talk about our various feelings. In time, we'll develop new and healthy pathways in our brain so we can think and feel at the same time.

The more we can talk about what has happened in a healthy, realistic way, the healthier we will become. We can talk to someone or vent alone when no one can hear us. We all talk to ourselves every day. The more we do this by ourselves and out loud, the greater impact this will have on our brain. It's one thing to think a new thought, but when we add the verbal, the thoughts also go through our listening abilities to the brain to create stronger pathways. The more this is done, the more our brain learns to use both sides simultaneously.[9]

The Benefits of Ritual

I've been asked so many times, "Will my traumatic memories go away?" The answer is no. They may seem to at times, but without assistance our emotional system is quiet. When the mending isn't there so we're not feeling the stretch, we might think, "Yes! It's gone. Hallelujah. I'm free!" And then one day our emotions are reactivated by some stimulus.

We can recognize our emotions better and diminish the pain. There can be freedom from the past. There can be freedom from the torment. One of the ways of controlling "yesterday trauma" is through rituals.

What is a ritual, and why does it work? When our past trauma surfaces in a flashback or intrusive memory, we may feel like we've been hit with a seizure. We're in chaos. "It's as though I'm reliving what happened. It comes out of the blue. Something triggers it. The unpredictability throws me. This element of surprise ruins my day."

What is ritual in this context? It's doing something purposeful and confronting the traumatic experience. It's taking charge. It's coming to the memories, confronting them, putting them in a time and place that we're in charge of. It's making the confrontation predictable and limiting its hold on us. We become the ones in charge.[10]

This is simply the process of facing our fear or trauma head-on. By doing this, we will regain control of our emotions and our lives and begin to gain some predictability about how we feel.[11] It's a step from living in the past to the present and the future.

What rituals might you engage in that will help your life at this time? Think about it, and pray specifically about it. Keep this in mind because it works: "Rituals mark and manage events. Rituals contain uncontainable emotions. They tell your emotional system to feel bad on this day so that you don't feel bad on all the others."[12] When you create a ritual you're creating a new pathway in your brain.

What Else Helps Us Heal?

Letter writing has been one of the healing steps for many, especially when we pray and ask God to prompt us with what to say and how to say it. There are many variations of letters. This suggestion may sound strange, but it may help to address the person we were when the trauma occurred. We might write to show how we've changed or highlight a positive quality we displayed during the crisis. We could write about what we did during the experience that we wish we hadn't. Another idea is to write to a body part that was impacted. Be as specific as possible. Ask God to reveal what may have been buried.

And then write a letter back from the traumatized person inside. When we write a letter like this, we need to be sure to include who or how we want to be at this time of our lives and our dreams for the future. Again, be as specific as possible.

I Wish I Could Tell You…

Another letter is "I Wish I Could Tell You." This is helpful for those who want to write but are hesitant to do so for one reason or another. Writing this letter removes the pressure of knowing it doesn't have to be sent.

We begin by sitting quietly for a few minutes. When we're ready, we'll take a moment to recall the person we are thinking about and consider what we would like to tell him or her if it were possible to do so:[13]

- What would my life be like if I no longer believed…?

- How happy would I feel if I no longer believed…?

- What could I accomplish if I no longer believed…?

Write out the answers to these questions.[14]

An Apology Letter

Another letter that has been helpful is an apology. This is not a letter in which we are apologizing; rather, it's a letter addressed to us *from* someone who hurt us.

First, we need to identify who the person is and then write it as if he or she were writing to us. Write the words we need to hear. It doesn't matter that this person might not respond in this way. This letter is for *our* benefit.

Writing this letter will help us if there's still denial over this painful past experience. Writing and reading the letter out loud confirms that we were hurt and we are aware of the fact. Leaving the denial state opens the door to forgiveness.[15]

An Autobiography

Another idea is to create an autobiography. What would be significant to include? For those of us who have experienced trauma, unfortunately, we tend to see the trauma as the only chapter of life that has significance. Have we considered what our lives would have been like if the trauma had not occurred? We could write about this. We can also create chapters for the present as well as the future. "What can we do about this now?"

There are some important steps to take. First of all, keep in mind that sending the letter is completely a choice. It helps to spend time and pray and gather our thoughts as well as feelings.

Don't worry about style, spelling, punctuation, and grammar. They can be fixed in a second draft if the letter will be sent.

We can share what we want the person to know about us and how the experience impacted our life. If we want something from them, we could write about that too. Remember, we don't have to mail this letter.

How do we begin? Just start writing and let the words flow. Order isn't important. Be specific and precise. Provide plenty of uninterrupted time to write. This is not a one-time experience. It's more productive when we leave the letter visible and available over a few days so we can return to it whenever anything else comes to mind. Keep the letter in an envelope where you know where it is, but no one else does or has access.

People write about their anger toward the person or what they did, the hurt they experienced toward what happened, and the fear and anxiety that were created. When any of these issues come back to mind, we can refuse it because we've written it out. It's out of us now. It's on the paper and in the envelope. We're free; we're not living in the past. Often one of the expressions in this letter is the extension of forgiveness to the person. Hurt and forgiveness often go hand in hand. The act of forgiveness is letting go of the hurt.

Using Your Letter

What do you do with the letter? Select a room that is private and somewhat soundproof, put two chairs facing one another, put the name of the "recipient" of the letter on a card on the one chair, and you sit in the other. Read the letter aloud with all the feeling you can generate. Listen to your voice say the words aloud. Some have found it beneficial to record their reading of the letter and play it back so they can hear it again and realize, "I am draining this material from within me. It's out. It's gone. It's on the paper and in the envelope." Remind yourself of this whenever the memories comes back. They have no hold on you anymore.

There may be a time when you want your letter to be given to the person you've written to. That is up to you and what you believe would be the most beneficial for both of you. If you send it, you might call them and let them know it's coming and what you hope to accomplish. You may want to meet with the person and read the letter to them. A variation of this would be to read the letter using Skype or Facetime. If you do this, be sure to give them a copy of the letter. Make sure you stay safe physically and emotionally.

The value of writing a letter is draining the content, the events, and the emotions from your life so you can move forward. You'll have the memories, but they will no longer control you. All you can accomplish by having the other person read or hear your letter is the fact that you've shared with them and you haven't just kept it to yourself. It doesn't matter whether the other person agrees with what you've said or not. If that is your goal, you will be disappointed as well as handing them some control of your life. They may argue or respond in a negative way. The other person may be incapable of accepting what you've said. Remember the purpose of this: purging what happened to you out of your mind and heart—letting go of past trauma.

Some have found it helpful to engage in a symbolic act after reading the letter aloud. Jamie described her experience:

> I went out to my backyard and sat under some wisteria. I sat there because the plant reminded me of something new and fragrant and also bringing new life to the day. I did this when no one was home, not even the neighbors. I read my letter twice. Once silently and then out loud with all the intensity I could muster. After I read it out loud, I needed a few minutes to calm down. I took several deep breaths and then said, "Goodbye, letter. Goodbye, hurt and anger. You served me well for years, but I no longer need you." I had several matches with me, and I took one and lit the letter. While it burned I said, "Goodbye, negative emotions! I release you. I give you away. I don't need you. I'm free. Jesus is covering me and my emotional life. He wants me to live now, not in the past. He is the source of my freedom."

As Jamie shared her story with me, tears fell from her eyes—not of sorrow, but of relief. She said, "I concluded this process by reading these passages out loud several times."

- "Cast your cares on the LORD and he will sustain you; he will never let the righteous be shaken" (Psalm 55:22).
- "God is our refuge and strength, an ever-present help in trouble" (Psalm 46:1).
- Cast all your anxiety on him because he cares for you" (1 Peter 5:7).

The act of burning the letter is a symbolic release. You see the pain, the suffering, and the bondage consumed by the flames.

What if the person you wrote to is no longer around? Taking it to the graveside and sharing it there is a very common and meaningful experience. Often it is helpful to take a friend with you for support. The reading of this letter will be the closing of a painful chapter and the opening of a new, healthy one. Read the letter aloud. It doesn't matter if this person will never know the contents. It's the writing and reading that is important. Be sure to state that you release all that has been within you that they were responsible for. When the reading is over, burn the letter and scatter the ashes. All of these suggestions can be helpful in handling intrusive thoughts.

Where Was God?

There is one other issue that needs to be addressed. It has to do with the foundation of healing, as well as faith. Many trauma survivors ask, "Where was God when these traumatic events occurred? Why wasn't He present? Why didn't He intervene?" Perhaps you've asked this or been hesitant to ask: "Does God not know or not care?"

Jesus shatters this question to smithereens. On the cross, He personally experienced the full range of human trauma: pain, injustice, abuse, betrayal, mockery, humiliation, powerlessness, physical abuse, thirst, and finally, death. We are not alone. God has written "I am with you" in His own blood.

In one of His dying gasps, Jesus said, "'*Eli, Eli, lema sabachthani?*' (which means 'My God, my God, why have you forsaken me?')" (Matthew 27:46). That cry, which is based on Psalm 22, is often called "the cry of dereliction." That's an accurate but shocking phrase. "Derelict" means something is forsaken, abandoned, cast away like a dog's carcass on the roadside. Where is God? Where was God? Why does God get off the hook? Is God sitting in His lounge chair watching, punishing, and turning His face away? No. Followers of Jesus say, "Look! There is our God...on a cross, suffering with us and for us." Jesus knew the dereliction of trauma. The Bible tells us, "[Jesus] was despised and rejected by mankind, a man of suffering, and familiar with pain" (Isaiah 53:3). Jesus Christ entered the brokenness of the world and all the brokenness of our lives. We love, and serve, and trust a God who understands trauma.[16] I urge you not to abandon your faith. Instead, renew it. It will change, and it will be tested. Listen to the words of Dr. Diane Langberg:

> What does trauma do to faith? Let me give you two things to keep in mind. The first is that trauma freezes thinking. Someone who has experienced trauma thinks about herself, her life, her relationships, and her future through the grid of the trauma. Trauma stops growth because it shuts everything down. It is of the nature of death. The thinking that grows out of the traumatic experience controls the input from new experiences. People who went to work every day [in the World Trade Center] and never thought about safety in the building or cared what floor they worked on will ponder such things daily. Some will decide to take a job or not based on what floor it is on. It will not matter that the vast majority of tall buildings in the world remain standing. The trauma will serve as the grid...
>
> Second, we learn about the unseen through the seen. We are of the earth, earthy. God teaches us truths through the world around us. We grasp a bit of eternity by looking at the sea. We get a glimmer of infinity by staring into space.

We learn about the shortness of time by the quickness of a vapor. Jesus taught this way. He said he was bread, light, water, and the vine. We look at the seen and learn about the unseen. Consider the sacraments—water, bread, and wine. We are taught about the holiest of all through the diet of a peasant. This method of pointing to the seen to teach about the unseen is used by God in teaching us about his character...

Many who suffered through [intense trauma] will struggle with the same two seemingly irreconcilable realities: God who is a refuge and trauma. Each seems to cancel out the other, yet both exist. The human mind can manage either alternative—trauma and no God, or God and no trauma. What is one to do with trauma *and* God?

The only answer to this dilemma...is the cross of Jesus Christ, for it is there that trauma and God come together. Perhaps I should say crash together. The components of trauma such as fear, helplessness, destruction, alienation, silence, loss, and hell have all been endured by Christ. He understands trauma. He willingly entered into trauma for us. He endured trauma abandoned by the Father so that we never have to be traumatized without the presence of the Father...

Jesus came in the flesh, explaining God to us. Jesus brought the unseen down into flesh and blood realities...The cross demonstrates the extent of the evil done. The cross demonstrates the extent of the love of God. The cross covers the failures of the suffering. The cross of Christ is God with us in our grief, our suffering, our trauma, and our sorrows.[17]

The last chapter of our trauma hasn't been written yet. And we can write that chapter. With God's help and presence, we will survive the storms of trauma.

Chapter 10

Trapped or Free?
We Choose

T rapped. That's exactly how I feel. I grew up trapped by my parents, trapped by where I lived, trapped by my life. I still feel trapped." I've talked with many who are living today as though it were still yesterday. They've carried their cages with them for most of their lives. You've probably seen animals caught in the wilds and then placed in cages. Most of them fight their confinement in a frantic way. They run from side to side and try to bite through the wire or bars. They growl and struggle to no avail. Eventually some of them give up and submit to their new, restricted life. The fight has gone out of them, and now they live in a state of despair and depression. For many people, the greatest prison is the brokenness of their minds. Traumatized, we act out the rehearsed scripts others have written.

A long time ago, in a small town in the British Isles, a new jail was constructed that claimed to have an escape-proof cell. Harry Houdini, the great escape artist known all over the world, was invited to come and test it to see if it really was escape-proof. He accepted the invitation, having once boasted that no jail could hold him.

Houdini entered the cell, and the jailer closed the door behind him. Houdini listened to the sound of the key being slipped into the lock. The jailer withdrew the key and left. Houdini took out his hidden tools and started the process of working on that cell door. But it didn't work out the way he'd expected. Nothing seemed to work, and the hours passed. He was puzzled because he'd never failed to open a locked door.

Finally the great Houdini admitted defeat. But when he leaned against the door in resigned exhaustion, it suddenly opened. The jailer had never locked it! The only place the door was locked was—you can guess—in Houdini's mind.

We've all done something similar. We locked ourselves in because of what we thought and believed. We allowed our minds to imprison us. As a result, we keep ourselves away from the hope and faith that's available to us. Instead of enjoying the assurance and freedom that comes from belonging to God, we become negative. We believe the bad things we tell ourselves or what others say about us. Nathaniel Hawthorne captured the dilemma beautifully in *The House of Seven Gables:* "What other dungeon is so dark as one's own heart! What jailer so inexorable as one's self!" We allow others and our past experiences to be our jailers.

What about it? Is there any event or person from your past you feel trapped by or who presently traps you? If it's a person, do you believe what they did was purposeful? Perhaps it was...or perhaps not. Consider the words of Jesus: "Father, forgive them, for they do not know what they are doing" (Luke 23:34). What would happen in your life if you believed and said what our Lord said: "Forgive them"? We assume the worst about others. Maybe what they did was on purpose. If we know Jesus as our personal Savior, we are forgiven and capable of learning to forgive others.[1]

Forgiveness is a condition in which the sins of the past are not altered or the inevitable consequences changed. In forgiveness, a fresh act is added to those of the past to restore the broken relationship and open the way for the one who forgives and the one who is forgiven to mesh and communicate deeply with each other in the present and future. Thus, forgiveness heals the past, though the scars remain and the consequences go on.[2]

Forgiveness boils down to this: We are forgiven people. We don't deserve to receive it. It is a gift from God that frees us and helps us be capable of forgiving those around us, whether we believe they deserve it or not. I like the way Jack Hayford describes this opportunity to move forward:

Forgive everyone—anyone—whom you think has failed you, hurt you, offended you. If you think they've done anything to ruin your day, ruin your life, ruin your opportunities, ruin your dreams, or block your goals—*forgive them*. Forgiving others is the key to living in the liberty of the freeing forgiveness Jesus has given us, and it's the first step toward finding hope for a hopeless day, not to mention opening the door to new days unimagined.[3]

When we feel trapped, we feel like a prisoner, and being in prison is not a pretty picture. It's a confined space with sterile, blank, cold walls. I've never been in one, but I've seen numerous pictures and portrayals in films. It's not an inviting place. I don't know of anyone who would choose to be there.

This prison isn't real. It exists in our minds and our emotions. We are not called to live a life of entrapment. God calls us to a life of hope. Consider the results of not experiencing hope: "Hope deferred makes the heart sick, but a longing fulfilled is a tree of life" (Proverbs 13:12). Without hope we suffer physically, emotionally, and spiritually. The loss of hope also imprisons us. King David struggled with this in his life. It's evident in his prayer:

> When my spirit was overwhelmed within me, You knew my path. In the way where I walk they have hidden a trap for me. Look to the right and see; for there is no one who regards me; there is no escape for me; no one cares for my soul…"*Bring my soul out of prison*, so that I may give thanks to Your name" (Psalm 142:3-4,7 NASB).

When we are able to leave our traps, our prisons of any kind, we live for today and tomorrow. "May the God of hope fill you with all joy and peace as you trust in him, so that you may overflow with hope by the power of the Holy Spirit" (Romans 15:13).

God's Word and Life—Our Choice

There are times when we end up being in prisons of our own making. As Galatians 5:1 declares, "It is for freedom that Christ has set us free. Stand firm, then, and do not let yourselves be burdened again by a yoke of slavery." Jesus desires to free us from our past and our heavy burdens. He loves and values us so much that He died and rose again to bring us that freedom. He is the author of true freedom. He is the one who can set us free.

Consider that God created us with the ability to choose right from wrong. We call it "free will." He cares so much for our freedom to choose that He will not interfere unless we ask. That is true love. *He wants us to choose life* through Jesus Christ, to truly be a new creature in Christ. Through Jesus our Lord, we can do what we could never do on our own (2 Corinthians 5:17; Galatians 2:20).

If we were victimized, it was not our fault. If our parents divorced, if someone abused us, if our parents rejected us, if we got laid off from our jobs—whatever the situation, if we did not choose it, we are not to blame. The way we *respond* to any situation, however, determines whether life is or isn't working for us and how much our past is still in control. We can't undo the past with all of its pain and hurt, but we can decide that we will no longer live as victims of the past.

There are forces over which we have no control that influence our lives and involve us in things happening to and around us. The factors are variable and change over time. But one thing is constant—how we *react* to our environment and the people around us. *We choose* how we approach our past and how we think about important issues and relationships today. The moral decline of society isn't our direct responsibility, but we are responsible for ourselves and what we teach others. If we're willing to learn, to grow, and to change, we will have more positive lives.

We all have weaknesses; we all have strengths. Some allow their strengths to dominate life; others allow their weaknesses to dominate. For some it's very apparent what their weaknesses are. For others, it may be hidden so well that it would take a mining expedition for it to be discovered. Some weak spots are temporary, while others are deeply rooted with a sense of permanency. We need to ask ourselves, "What keeps me where I don't want to be or impairs my relationships in some way?"

Achilles' Heel

"Achilles' heel" comes from the Greek myth of the great warrior Achilles. According to legend, when Achilles' mother dipped him in the river Styx to make him invulnerable, the water washed every part except the heel by which she held him. That one weak spot—his heel—was the proof of his humanity and his greatest weakness. Rather than accepting his vulnerability and learning from it, Achilles always tried to prove he was invincible. In battles he repeatedly exposed himself to attack. He won several battles before his rival shot an arrow into his heel and killed him.

Our Achilles' heel is the part of ourselves that is our greatest handicap and our greatest challenge. If we can accept and learn from our weakness, we can turn it into a source of power, a stimulus to growth, an essential part of our humanity. The irony of the Achilles story is that the mighty warrior had only three inches of weakness, but those three inches became his downfall. Like Achilles, many of us measure our lives by our weaknesses, as if that was who we are.[4]

There are many events in my life that I never anticipated. The office of the American–Arab Anti-Discrimination League was 100 yards from my counseling office. One day when I wasn't working, that office was blown up by a terrorist bomb and the director was killed. I saw the results on television. I never expected that an office next to mine would be blown up. But it happened.

I never expected a business associate to mismanage the running of my business to the extent that I would almost lose everything. But it happened.

I never expected that on one of my outings as youth director, a high-school boy would fall over a 400-foot cliff to his death. It happened. I watched as they carried him out in a body bag on the back of a horse.

I never expected that one of my children would take a detour in her Christian life. But it happened and continued for years.

I never expected to have my only son be born with profound brain damage and die suddenly at the age of twenty-two. But it happened.

I never expected that my wife, Joyce, would have a malignant tumor and die four years later. But it happened.

And I never expected my 53-year-old daughter to die during the writing of this book. But she did.

Over the years, my wife and I have learned the truth and significance of many passages from God's Word. One passage in particular came alive as we depended on it more and more: "Consider it all joy, my brethren, when you encounter various trials, knowing that the testing of your faith produces endurance. And let endurance have its perfect result, so that you may be perfect and complete, lacking in nothing" (James 1:2-4 NASB). The Amplified Version puts it this way: "Consider it nothing but joy, my brothers and sisters, whenever you fall into various trials. Be assured that the testing of your faith [through experience] produces endurance [leading to spiritual maturity, and inner peace]. And let endurance have its perfect result and do a thorough work, so that you may be perfect and completely developed [in your faith], lacking in nothing" (brackets in original).

Learning to put this attitude into practice is a *process*. The passage doesn't say, "Respond this way immediately." We have to feel the pain and grief first, and then with God's help we'll be able to consider it joy.

What does the word "consider" mean? As I studied commentaries, I discovered that the word refers to *an internal attitude of the heart or mind that allows the trial and circumstance of life to affect us either adversely or beneficially.* We could say, "Make up your mind to regard adversity as something to welcome or be glad about."

We have the power to decide what our attitude will be. We can say about a trial, "That's terrible. Totally upsetting. That's the last thing I wanted for my life. Why did it have to happen now? Why me?" Or we can say, "It's not what I wanted or expected, but it's here. There are going to be some difficult times. How can I make the most of them?" "Consider" indicates a decisiveness of action. It's not an attitude of resignation. It's not, "Well, I just give up. I'm stuck with this problem. That's the way life is." We resign ourselves to the season and sit back and do nothing.

But James 1:2 indicates that we're to go against our natural inclination in order to see the trial as a positive occurrence. There will be some moments when we'll have to remind ourselves to think of a better way of responding. We need to say, "Lord, I really want You to help me see this from Your perspective." Then our minds will shift to more constructive responses.

Yes, this often takes a lot of work. But discovering and implementing God's perspective enables us to look beyond the present and the past. And that is the ultimate survival tool.

Remember, the greater the loss and the worse the trauma, the longer the recovery will take. God created us with the capacity and the freedom to decide how we will respond to the unexpected incidents life brings our way. We may wish certain events never occurred, but we can't change the fact that they did. So always choose hope.

"Resilience" is the ability to bounce back and recover from a loss, or trauma, or any setback. My dictionary equates it with elasticity: "the ability to spring back quickly into shape after being bent, stretched, or deformed." It may seem almost magical when we can restore to wholeness what has been misshapen, when what was buckled and bowed becomes straight again. Without resilience, we would be very deformed.[5] If it weren't for resilience and the process of repair, we couldn't open our lives again, we couldn't risk again, we couldn't love again.

One analogy used to describe traumatic states is that of a river that has become blocked by debris. When the water is not flowing freely, it disturbs life. Parts that are blocked become starved of life, while parts that are flooded are endangered in another way.[6]

We also have a choice to forgive those involved in our pain. We choose to believe that forgiveness brings healing. Those who choose to languish in the pit of unforgiveness allow bitterness to take root in their hearts. In this dark place, the light of truth can barely be seen. It's more than *self-pity*, for it is a prison we lock ourselves into if we don't seek help from God and the people available to us.

The hopelessness of a human soul, the shallow look in the eye, the resigned defeat of the spirit of a man or woman are only temporary if that person is serious about healing. We need to develop the mindset that where we are today is only temporary. The future is bright for those who take hold of God's healing grace and then share it with others. Paul wrote:

I want to know Christ—yes, to know the power of his resurrection and participation in his sufferings, becoming like
him in his death, and so, somehow,
attaining to the resurrection from
the dead. Not that I have already
obtained all this, or have already
arrived at my goal, but I press on to
take hold of that for which Christ
Jesus took hold of me. Brothers and
sisters, I do not consider myself yet to have taken hold of it.
But one thing I do: Forgetting what is behind and straining
toward what is ahead, I press on toward the goal to win the
prize for which God has called me heavenward in Christ
Jesus (Philippians 3:10-14).

> The greater the
> loss...the longer the
> recovery will take.

Duncan Sinclair wrote:

> It is clear to Paul and us that hope is a key to life. Without
> hope in living there is no reason for being. To "forget what is
> behind me and do my best to reach what is ahead" may well
> be the goal for many; however, when that which is behind
> presents itself continually in the present—and with inten-
> sity and cruelty—then the process is shifted. When this pro-
> cess of hope is shut down and no longer functions, there is
> a severe spiritual crisis. It is this crisis of the loss of hope that
> calls our attention to the seriousness of the trauma.[7]

Did you catch that one sentence? "When that which is behind pres-
ents itself continually in the present...then the process is shifted." Are
you feeling the loss of hope? You may have been rejected as a child. You
may have outlived all of your friends and family. You may be alienated by
society and living in prison. But your life is still a gift. You are a victor, not
a victim. A conqueror, not a loser. You may not believe that, but you are.
You're going through a refining fire, and you will come out like silver.[8]

Who We Are in Christ

> Because of Christ's redemption,
> I am a new creation of infinite worth.
> I am deeply loved,
> I am completely forgiven,
> I am totally pleasing,
> I am totally accepted by God,
> I am absolutely complete in Christ.
> When my performance
> Reflects my new identity in Christ,
> That reflection is dynamically unique.
> There has never been another person like me
> In the history of mankind,
> Nor will there ever be.
> God has made me an original,
> One of a kind,
> A special person.[9]

You have been declared someone special—and you are! As Scripture says:

> Even before he made the world, God loved us and chose us in Christ to be holy and without fault in his eyes. God decided in advance to adopt us into his own family by bringing us to himself through Jesus Christ. This is what he wanted to do, and it gave him great pleasure (Ephesians 1:4-5 NLT).

What are some of the rights and privileges we inherited? The book of Ephesians lists many of them.

- We have been guaranteed eternal life, so evidenced by the presence of the Holy Spirit in our lives (1:13-14).
- We have hope in Christ, our "glorious inheritance" (1:18).
- We have experienced the incomparable power that raised

Jesus Christ from the dead and seated Him at God's right hand (1:19-20).

- We are the recipient of God's incomparable grace that saved us apart from anything we have done well or will ever do (2:8-9).
- We now have access to the Father by the Holy Spirit (2:18).
- We can know the love of Christ, which will enable us to receive God's holiness (3:18-19).

You and I are rich despite the pain from our pasts. We don't want to let the past have power and control over us. We do want to let the Word of God be alive in our lives. One of the men who has influenced and blessed me for years is Max Lucado. Read each word of this passage from his book *You'll Get Through This* aloud. Let the truth of his words and Scripture sink into your heart and mind:

> *You'll get through this.* You fear you won't. We all do. We fear that the depression will never lift, the yelling will never stop, the pain will never leave. We wonder, *Will this gray sky ever brighten? This load ever lighten?* We feel stuck, trapped, locked in. Predestined for failure.
>
> Out of the lions' den for Daniel, the prison for Peter, the whale's belly for Jonah, Goliath's shadow for David, the storm for the disciples, disease for the lepers, doubt for Thomas, the grave for Lazarus, and the shackles for Paul. God gets us through stuff. *Through* the Red Sea onto solid ground (Exodus 14:22), *through* the wilderness (Deuteronomy 29:5), *through* the valley of the shadow of death (Psalm 23:4), and *through* the deep sea (Psalm 77:19). *Through* is a favorite word of God's:
>
>> When you pass *through* the waters, I will be with you; and *through* the rivers, they shall not overflow you. When you walk *through* the fire, you shall not be burned, Nor shall the flame scorch you (Isaiah 43:2).

It won't be painless. Does God guarantee the absence of struggle and the abundance of strength? Not in this life. But he does pledge to reweave your pain for a higher purpose.

It won't be quick. How long will God take with you? He may take his time. His history is redeemed not in minutes but in lifetimes.

But God will use your mess for good. We see a perfect mess; God sees a perfect chance to train, test, and teach you.

The stories in the Bible are there for a reason: to teach you to trust God to trump evil. What Satan intends for evil, God, the Master Weaver and Master Builder, redeems for good.[10]

You have your story. Tell it to Jesus. Let Him have your story, and let Him change your life. And then share His truths with joy and conviction.

Notes

Chapter 1—Are We Our Past?

1. Pete Wilson, *Let Hope In* (Nashville: Word, 2013), 77-78.
2. Jimmy Evans and Ann Billington, *Freedom from Your Past* (Dallas: Marriage Today, 2009), xiii-xiv.
3. David Hart, PhD, "The Path to Wholeness," *Psychological Perspective* (Fall 1972), 152.
4. Jerry Sittser, *A Grace Revealed* (Grand Rapids, MI: Zondervan, 2012), 137, adapted.
5. Sittser, *Grace Revealed*, 155.
6. Sittser, *Grace Revealed*, 155.
7. Sittser, *Grace Revealed*, 160-61.
8. Sidney B. Simon, PhD, and Suzanne Simon, *Forgiveness: How to Make Peace with Your Past and Get On with Your Life* (New York: Grand Central Publishing, 1990), 92-93.
9. Simon and Simon, *Forgiveness,* 56.
10. Stephen Viars, *Putting Your Past in Its Place* (Eugene, OR: Harvest House, 2011), 66-67, adapted.
11. Viars, *Putting Your Past in Its Place,* 47-48.
12. Wilson, *Let Hope In*, 10-11, adapted.
13. Simon and Simon, *Forgiveness,* 70-72, adapted.
14. Pat Layton, *Life Unstuck* (Grand Rapids, MI: Revell, 2015), quoting H. Norman Wright, *Making Peace with Your Past* (Grand Rapids, MI: Revell, 1984), 9.
15. Layton, *Life Unstuck*, quoting A.W. Tozer, *The Pursuit of God*, definitive classic ed. (Ventura, CA: Regal, 2013), 19.
16. Layton, *Life Unstuck*, 87-88, adapted.
17. Darcy L. Harris, *Counting Our Losses* (New York: Routledge, 2011), 5-9, adapted.

Chapter 2—Memories

1. Robert D. Jones, *Bad Memories—Getting Past Your Past* (Phillipsburg, NJ: P & R Publishing, 2004), 4-5.
2. N. Duncan Sinclair, *Horrific Traumata* (New York: Haworth Pastoral, 1993), 70.
3. Curt Thompson, MD, *Anatomy of the Soul* (Wheaton, IL: Tyndale House, 2010), 83.
4. David Ziegler, *Traumatic Experience and the Brain* (Gilbert, AZ: Acacia Publishing, 2004), 32, adapted.
5. *The Brain: The Ultimate Guide* (New York: Harris Publishing, 2015), 31, adapted.
6. Thompson, *Anatomy of the Soul*, 76.
7. Laura Davis, *I Thought We'd Never Speak Again* (New York: Harper, 2003), 7.
8. George Kuykendall, "Care for the Dying: A Kubler-Ross Critique," *Theology Today,* 38 (April

1981), 45, http://theologytoday.ptsem.edu/apr.1981/v38-1article4.htm, quoted in Albert Y. Hsu, *Grieving a Suicide* (Downers Grove, IL: IVP Books, 2002), 69.

9. Albert Y. Hsu, *Grieving a Suicide* (Downers Grove, IL: IVP Books, 2002), 69.

10. Frederick Buechner, *A Room Called Remember* (San Francisco: Harper, 1992), 8.

11. Buechner, *Room Called Remember*, 4.

12. Max Lucado, *God Came Near* (Nashville: Thomas Nelson, 2013), portions taken from 87-89.

13. Thompson, *Anatomy of the Soul*, 85-87, adapted.

14. Mandy Evans, *Traveling Free* (Desert Hot Springs, CA: Yes You Can Press, 1990), 24.

15. Hsu, *Grieving a Suicide*, 70.

16. David Seamands, *Healing of Memories* (Wheaton, IL: Victor Books, 1985), 186-87.

17. Thompson, *Anatomy of the Soul* , 81.

18. Thompson, *Anatomy of the Soul* , 79-80, adapted.

19. Buechner, *Room Called Remember*, 12.

20. Michael Leuing, *A Common Prayer* (New York: HarperCollins, 1991).

21. Ron Mehl, "God Works the Night Shift," taken from *God Works the Night Shift* (Sisters, OR: Multnomah, 1994).

Chapter 3—We Are Our Thoughts

1. H. Norman Wright, *A Better Way to Think* (Grand Rapids, MI: Revell, 2011), 27, adapted.

2. Earl Lee, *Recycle for Living* (Ventura, CA: Regal Books, 1973), 4.

3. Caroline Leaf, PhD, *Who Switched Off My Brain?* (Dallas: Switch on Your Brain, Inc., 2008), 9-10, adapted.

4. Leaf, *Who Switched Off My Brain?*, introduction, adapted.

5. Shad Helmstetter, *The Self-Talk Solution* (New York: Pocket Books, 1987), 85-89.

6. John Selby, *Quiet Your Mind* (Maui: Inner Ocean Publishing, 2004), 12-15, adapted.

7. Gregory L. Jantz, PhD, with Ann McMurray, *Moving Beyond Depression* (Colorado Springs: Shaw Books, 2003), 15-16.

8. D. Martyn Lloyd-Jones, *Studies on the Sermon on the Mount* (Grand Rapids, MI: Eerdmans Publishing Company, 1984), 289, adapted.

9. Mark G. Karris, *Borrowing Hope: A Path to Healing a Broken Heart*, mss.

10. A.B. Curtiss, *Brain Switch Out of Depression* (Escondido, CA: Old Castle Publishing, 2011), 55-60, adapted.

11. Curtiss, *Brain Switch Out of Depression*, 96.

12. Curtiss, *Brain Switch Out of Depression*, 19, 48, adapted.

13. Tommy Walker, *He Knows My Name* (Ventura, CA: Regal, 2004), 185.

14. Robert S. McGee, *The Search for Significance,* rev. ed. (Nashville: W Publishing Group, 2003), 266.

Chapter 4—Emotions and Life—Especially Anger

1. Sidney B. Simon, PhD, and Suzanne Simon, *Forgiveness: How to Make Peace with Your Past and Get On with Your Life* (New York: Grand Central Publishing, 1990), 37.

2. Simon and Simon, *Forgiveness*, 46.

3. Simon and Simon, *Forgiveness*, 43.

4. Paul Welter, *Family Problems and Predicaments* (Wheaton, IL: Tyndale House Publishers, 1977), 130.

5. Gary Oliver, PhD, and H. Norman Wright, PhD, *When Anger Hits Home* (Chicago: Moody Press, 1992), excerpts from 62-65, 68-69, 71.

6. Nancy Napier, *Getting Through the Day* (New York: W.W. Norton & Co., 1994), 122, adapted.

7. *The Brain: The Ultimate Guide* (New York: Harris Publishing, 2015), 63, 65, adapted.

8. Glenn Schiraldi, *Post-Traumatic Stress Disorder Sourcebook* (New York: McGraw-Hill, 2009), 142, adapted.

9. David Viscott, *I Love You, Let's Work It Out* (New York: Simon & Schuster, 1987), 67.

10. Carol Staudacher, *Beyond Grief: A Guide for Recovering from the Death of a Loved One* (Oakland, CA: New Harbinger, 1987), 30-31, adapted.

11. Pete Wilson, *Let Hope In* (Nashville: Word, 2013), 17.

12. Byron Brown, *Soul Without Shame* (Boston, MA: Shambhala, 1998), 14.

13. David Viscott, *Emotionally Free* (Chicago: Contemporary Books, 1992), 2-3.

14. Viscott, *Emotionally Free*, 3.

Chapter 5—Fear vs. Hope

1. Sidney Simon, PhD, *Getting Unstuck* (New York: Warner Books, 1988), 175-79, adapted.

2. John Haggai, *How to Win over Fear* (Eugene, OR: Harvest House, 1987), 73.

3. Lee Strobel, *What Jesus Would Say* (Grand Rapids, MI: Zondervan, 1994), 161.

4. Albert Y. Hsu, *Grieving a Suicide* (Downers Grove, IL: IVP Books, 2002), 134.

5. Paul L. Walker, *Courage for Crisis Living* (Grand Rapids, MI: Fleming H. Revell, 1978), 29.

6. Theresa Rhodes McGee, *Transforming Trauma* (Maryknoll, KY: Orbis Books, 2005), 16-17.

7. H. Norman Wright, *Overcoming Fear & Worry* (Torrance, CA: Rose Publishing, 2014), 27.

8. Wright, *Overcoming Fear & Worry*, 27.

9. Gregory L. Jantz with Ann McMurray, *Overcoming Anxiety, Worry and Fear: Practical Ways to Find Peace* (Grand Rapids, MI: Revell, 2011), 125, adapted.

10. Frederick Buechner, *A Room Called Remember* (San Francisco: Harper, 1992), 11.

Chapter 6—Our Brain

1. *The Brain: The Ultimate Guide* (New York: Harris Publishing, 2015), 7, 27, adapted.

2. Heather Davediuk Gingrich, PhD, *Restoring the Shattered Self: A Christian Counselor's Guide to Complex Trauma* (Downers Grove, IL: IVP Academic, 2013), 38-39, adapted.

3. Bessel van der Kolk, MD, *The Body Keeps Score* (New York: Viking, 2014), 255, adapted.

4. Van der Kolk, *Body Keeps Score*, 44, adapted.

5. Judith Herman, *Trauma and Recovery* (New York: Basic Books, 1982), 42-43, adapted.

6. Van der Kolk, *Body Keeps Score*, 52.

7. David J. Morris, *The Evil Hours* (Chicago: Eamon Dolan/Mariner Books, 2016), 56-57.

8. Diane Langberg, "Coping with Traumatic Memory," paper presented at The Soul Care Trauma Response and Intervention Project (TRIP) conference, New York, NY, October 2001.

9. Van der Kolk, *Body Keeps Score,* adapted.

10. Michael J. Scott, *Moving on After Trauma* (New York: Routledge, 2008), 23-25, adapted.

11. Herman, *Trauma and Recovery,* 47.

12. Laurence Gonzales, *Surviving Survival* (New York: W.W. Norton & Co., 2012), 25-27, adapted.

13. Van der Kolk, *Body Keeps Score,* 80, adapted.

14. Van der Kolk, *Body Keeps Score,* 61-64, adapted.

15. Morris, *Evil Hours,* 47, adapted.

16. Herman, *Trauma and Recovery,* 47, adapted.

17. Dana Foundation, *Cerebrum 2008, Emerging Ideas on Brain Science* (New York: Dana Press, 2008), 191-93, adapted.

18. Chuck Swindoll, *Living Above the Level of Mediocrity* (Dallas: Word, 1987), 94-95.

Chapter 7—Grieving Past Losses

1. Ronald W. Ramsey, PhD, and Rene Noorbergen, *Living with Loss* (New York: William Morrow & Co., 1981), 47-48, adapted.

2. This poem came in response to an anonymous survey I conducted some years ago.

3. R Scott Sullender, *Grief and Growth* (New York: Paulist Press, 1985), 96-101, adapted.

4. Therese A. Rando, *Grieving: How to Go on Living When Someone You Love Dies* (Lexington, MA: Lexington Books, 1988), 11-12, adapted.

5. Rando, *Grieving,* 18-19, adapted.

6. Bob Diets, *Life After Loss* (Tucson, AZ: Fisher Books, 1988), 27, adapted.

7. Albert Y. Hsu, *Grieving a Suicide* (Downers Grove, IL: IVP Books, 2002), 89.

8. Diets, *Life After Loss,* 28.

9. Peter Walker, *Complex PTSD: From Surviving to Thriving* (CreateSpace Independent Publishing, a Division of Amazon Group, www.CreateSpace.com, 2013), 217-18, adapted.

10. Walker, *Complex PTSD,* 218, adapted.

11. Joyce Rupp, *Praying Our Goodbyes* (New York: Ivy Books, 1988), 7-8, adapted.

12. Rupp, *Praying Our Goodbyes,* 20-21.

13. Lewis Smedes, *Forgive and Forget* (New York: Harper & Row, 1984), 37.

14. Jerry Sittser, *A Grace Disguised* (Grand Rapids, MI: Zondervan, 1998), 86-91, adapted.

15. William Bridges, *The Way of Transitions: Embracing Life's Most Difficult Moments* (Cambridge, MA: Perseus, 2001), 21, adapted.

16. Hsu, *Grieving a Suicide,* 130.

17. Darcy L. Harris, *Counting Our Losses* (New York: Routledge, 2011), 5-8, adapted.

Chapter 8—Trauma and Our Past

1. Joan Hunter, *Freedom Beyond Comprehension* (New Kensington, PA: Whitaker House, 2012), ch. 1.

2. Bessel van der Kolk, MD, *The Body Keeps Score* (New York: Viking, 2014), 256, adapted.

3. David J. Morris, *The Evil Hours* (Chicago: Eamon Dolan/Mariner Books, 2016), xii, adapted.

4. Hunter, *Freedom Beyond Comprehension.*

5. N. Duncan Sinclair, *Horrific Traumata* (New York: Haworth Pastoral, 1993), 52-53, adapted.

6. Van der Kolk, *Body Keeps Score,* 46, adapted.

7. Ronald A. Ruden, *When the Past Is Always Present* (New York: Rutledge, 2011), 1, 11, adapted.

8. Morris, *Evil Hours,* 44.

9. Van der Kolk, *Body Keeps Score,* 198.

10. Heather Davediuk Gingrich, *Restoring the Shattered Self: A Christian Counselor's Guide to Complex Trauma* (Downers Grove, IL: IVP Academic, 2013), 16, adapted.

11. Caroline Leaf, PhD, *Who Switched Off My Brain?* (Dallas: Switch on Your Brain, Inc., 2008), 97, adapted.

12. Pete Walker, *Complex PTSD: From Surviving to Thriving* (CreateSpace Independent Publishing Platform, 2013), 3-4.

13. Dave Ziegler, *Traumatic Experience and the Brain* (Phoenix: Acacia Publishing, 2002), 42-43, adapted.

14. Walker, *Complex PTSD,* adapted, 11-13; *Complex Trauma* by C.A. Courtois, PhD, 1-2, adapted.

15. Diane Langberg, PhD, *Counseling Survivors of Sexual Abuse* (Wheaton, IL: Tyndale House, 2003), 51, adapted.

16. Langberg, *Counseling Survivors of Sexual Abuse,* 45, adapted.

17. Theresa Rhodes McGee, *Transforming Trauma* (Maryknoll, KY: Orbis Books, 2005), 32.

18. Van der Kolk, *Body Keeps Score,* 96.

19. McGee, *Transforming Trauma,* adapted.

20. Dena Rosenbloom, PhD, and Mary Beth Williams, PhD, with Barbara E. Watkins, *Life After Trauma* (New York: Guilford Press, 1999), 48-49, adapted.

21. Michael Scott, *Moving on After Trauma* (New York: Routledge, 2008), 70-71, adapted.

22. McGee, *Transforming Trauma,* 34-35.

23. Sinclair, *Horrific Traumata,* 69, adapted.

Chapter 9—Putting Past Trauma Behind Us

1. Terene Monmaney, "For Most Trauma Victims Life Is More Meaningful," *Los Angeles Times* (October 7, 2001), 9, citing research from Richard Tedeschi, University of North Carolina; Dr. Robert Ursano, Uniformed Services University of the Health Sciences (Bethesda, MD), Dr. Sandra Bloom.

2. Harriet Hill, Margaret Hill, Richard Bagge, Pat Miersma, *Healing the Wounds of Trauma: How the Church Can Help* (New York: American Bible Society, 2013), 82-84, adapted.

3. Pete Walker, *Complex PTSD* (CreateSpace Independent Publishing Platform, 2013), 61, adapted.

4. Albert Y. Hsu, *Grieving a Suicide* (Downers Grove, IL: IVP Books, 2002), 46.

5. Curt Thompson, MD, *Anatomy of the Soul* (Wheaton, IL: Tyndale House, 2010), 81.

6. H. Norman Wright and Matt and Julie Woodley, *Finding Hope When Life Goes Wrong* (Grand Rapids, MI: Revell, 2012), 110-11, 114-17, 121-22, adapted.

7. Pete Walker, "Grieving and Complex PTSD," http://pete-walker.com/pdf/GrievingAndCom plexPTSD.pdf.

8. Walker, *Complex PTSD*, 230-31, adapted.

9. Walker, *Complex PTSD*, 222-36, adapted.

10. Laurence Gonzales, *Surviving Survival* (New York: W.W. Norton & Co., 2012), 116, 124, adapted.

11. Gonzales, *Surviving Survival*, 215, adapted.

12. Gonzales, *Surviving Survival*, 116.

13. Susan Borkin, *The Healing Power of Writing* (New York: W.W. Norton, 2014), 117.

14. Borkin, *Healing Power of Writing*, 59, adapted.

15. Sidney B. Simon, PhD, and Suzanne Simon, *Forgiveness: How to Make Peace with Your Past and Get On with Your Life* (New York: Grand Central Publishing, 1990), 96-98, adapted.

16. Wright and Woodley, *Finding Hope When Life Goes Wrong*, 132-33, adapted.

17. Diane Mundt Langberg, "Coping with Traumatic Memory," *Marriage & Family: A Christian Journal* , no. 4 (2002), 447, 454-55.

Chapter 10—Trapped or Free? We Choose

1. Jack Hayford, *Hope for a Hopeless Day* (Ventura, CA: Regal Books, 2001), 25-26, adapted.

2. Amy Lyles Wilson, *Give: Perspectives on Making Peace with Your Past* (Vancouver, BC: Fresh Air Publishing, 2008), 11, adapted.

3. Hayford, *Hope for a Hopeless Day*, 35.

4. Harold H. Bloomfield, MD, *Making Peace with Yourself* (New York: Ballantine Books, 1985), 2, 14, adapted.

5. Jasmin Lee Cori, MS, LPC, *Healing from Trauma* (New York: Marlowe and Company, 2008), 20, adapted.

6. Cori, *Healing from Trauma*, 20-21, adapted.

7. Duncan Sinclair, *Horrific Traumata* (New York: Haworth Pastoral, 1993), 97-98.

8. H. Norman Wright and Larry Renetsky, *Healing Grace* (Ventura, CA: Regal Books, 2007), 26-31, adapted.

9. Robert S. McGee, *The Search for Significance*, rev. ed. (Nashville: W Publishing Group, 1998, 2003), 266.

10. Max Lucado, *You'll Get Through This* (Philadelphia, PA: Running Press, 2015), 8-10, emphasis in original.

Great Harvest House Books by
H. Norman Wright

101 Questions to Ask Before You Get Engaged

101 Questions to Ask Before You Get Remarried

101 Ways to Build a Stronger, More Exciting Marriage

After You Say "I Do"

After You Say "I Do" Devotional

Before You Remarry

Before You Say "I Do"®

Before You Say "I Do"® Devotional

Before You Say "I Do"™ DVD

Coping with Chronic Illness

Finding the Right One for You

*Helping Your Kids Deal with Anger, Fear,
and Sadness (ebook only)*

Quiet Times for Couples

Quiet Times for Every Parent (ebook only)

Quiet Times for Those Who Need Comfort (ebook only)

Reflections of a Grieving Spouse

Strong to the Core (Devotional, ebook only)

Success over Stress

Truly Devoted (Dogs)

What to Say When You Don't Know What to Say

Winning over Your Emotions

Quiet Times for Couples

*"Let Norman Wright guide you together to God...
and your marriage will never be the same."*
MAX LUCADO

**Uplifting, insightful devotions that will inspire,
encourage, and strengthen your marriage**

In these short devotions that promote togetherness, joy, and sharing your
dreams, trusted Christian counselor and bestselling author Norm Wright
offers...

- innovative ideas to establish and maintain a flourishing
  marriage
- insights for encouraging intimacy and harmony
- little and big things you can do to enhance your relationship
- specific suggestions for accommodating differences and handling conflicts
- great ideas for supporting and helping your spouse

Your relationship will become more loving, considerate, and united as the
two of you experience these quiet "together times" filled with deep insights,
powerful meditations, God's presence, and His truths and love.

Strong to the Core

*Men, strengthen Your Heart, Mind, and Spirit
in Just 5 Minutes a Day!*

Bestselling author Norm Wright has a proven plan to help you strengthen your core—your spiritual life, your family life, and your personal life. In these short devotions you'll find biblical truth, wisdom for growing your relationships, and time-tested advice for handling temptations and working through problems.

Professional knowledge coupled with practical insights garnered through Norm's many years as a respected Christian counselor will help you…

- increase your understanding of the Lord and His will
- communicate more effectively in relationships, especially marriage
- strengthen your reliance on God and His Word
- develop traits that reveal your heart for God
- implement your faith and God-given gifts to help others

Strong to the Core encourages you to embrace God's call to live for Him, represent Him, and take a stand for Him. You can make a difference!

Success over Stress

Isn't it time to take back your life?

You can't eliminate all stress, but you can certainly lessen its negative impact. Noted Christian counselor Norm Wright shares the action steps that have enabled thousands of people to find greater happiness, satisfaction, and peace. Through true, encouraging stories, biblical wisdom, and practical suggestions, you'll discover how to decrease your stressors by:

- simplifying your work and home life
- releasing any emotional baggage
- taking control of your schedule and finances
- establishing livable goals and priorities
- experiencing God's presence more fully

Packed with sound advice and proven steps for handling worry, fear, irritation, and more, *Success over Stress* reveals how you can experience more joy, energy, and satisfaction every day.

Truly Devoted

What Dogs Teach Us About Life,
Love, and Loyalty

Packed with dog adventures and antics that will make you smile, these devotions by trusted counselor Norm Wright provide warmhearted insights for improving your relationships with the people in your life. Drawing on wisdom from God's Word, many years of helping people, and time spent working with his beloved dogs, Norm encourages you to...

- explore how you can share God's faithfulness and comfort
- understand God through the world around you
- relax and enjoy the amazing love God offers
- meet with God every day
- draw strength, faith, and patience from His Word

As you glimpse some of the joys and quirks of four-legged family members, you'll discover surprising ideas that will help you draw closer to God, live vibrantly, and experience more fulfilling connections with family and friends.

To learn more about Harvest House books and
to read sample chapters, visit our website:

www.harvesthousepublishers.com

HARVEST HOUSE PUBLISHERS
EUGENE, OREGON